Developing
Corporate Character

Alan L. Wilkins

Developing
Corporate Character

How to Successfully
Change an Organization
Without Destroying It

Jossey-Bass Publishers
San Francisco • London • 1989

DEVELOPING CORPORATE CHARACTER
How to Successfully Change an Organization Without Destroying It
by Alan L. Wilkins

Library of Congress Cataloging-in-Publication Data

Wilkins, Alan L., date
    Developing corporate character : how to successfully change an
organization without destroying it / Alan L. Wilkins.
        p.   cm. — (The Jossey-Bass management series)
    Bibliography: p.
    Includes index.
    ISBN 1-55542-133-4
    1. Organizational change. 2. Organizational effectiveness.
I. Title. II. Series.
HD58.8.W54   1989
658.4'063—dc19   88-26698
                                                                         CIP

Manufactured in the United States of America

The paper in this book meets the guidelines for
permanence and durability of the Committee on
Production Guidelines for Book Longevity of the
Council on Library Resources.

JACKET DESIGN BY WILLI BAUM

FIRST EDITION

Code 8906

The Jossey-Bass
Management Series

Consulting Editors
Organizations and Management

Warren Bennis
University of Southern California

Richard O. Mason
Southern Methodist University

Ian I. Mitroff
University of Southern California

80001

Contents

Preface

Too many managers have tried to change their organization's culture and have succeeded only in destroying the character of their organization. The purpose of *Developing Corporate Character* is to examine why so many attempts at change have failed and to suggest what successful efforts have done differently. Unfortunately, organizational culture usually takes some time to change. Hence, hard lessons about failure and success have been slow to become clear.

The most important point I want to make is that those who are trying to create a new organizational future must also honor the past. Too many executives and managers who have restructured or tried to change organizational culture have announced bold new visions and significant layoffs in the same breath. They have often impressed shareholders in the short term only to find that employees who are left have no faith in either the new vision or the company's ability to implement it. My intent in this book is to describe how successful managers and executives have been able to deal with this very crucial tension—how they encourage employee faith in the fairness and ability of the organization and also involve employees in envisioning a new future and in developing new skills to implement that vision.

I use the term *character* rather than *culture* for several reasons that are related to why we have so often failed at cultural change in organizations. First, culture has been trivialized because so many have written about "managing culture," "managing myths," or "creating meaning" without serious attention

xi

to just how difficult it is to manipulate these complex social processes. Second, culture has been used to talk about almost everything organizational, and it has therefore lost much of its special meaning.

The idea that organizations have a character has a number of advantages. It helps us remember that change is best thought of as development and growth. We develop character; we do not change character. And when we do change character, we are, as often as not, out of character, acting out parts that we cannot legitimately support with real skills and internalized values. Organizational character is the result of the development of good habits through self-disciplined practice. The essence of a firm's competitive advantage is its character, its distinctive skills. And these skills cannot be announced in a vision statement or imported through merger. Distinctive skills have to be grown incrementally.

Character is not just something an individual or an organization has. It is also an earned reputation—an image in a larger community. This connotation helps us to understand that development of character requires renegotiating reputation or role with both outside and inside constituencies. Consistency and integrity in relationships with others are the source of a particular reputation. Hence, organizations have to earn the right to announce a new vision for their role before others accept that new role.

If corporate character is to be maintained or improved, past commitments must be kept or renegotiated in good faith. My intention in using *corporate character* to talk about change and development in the distinctive competence of organizations is (1) to show what we lose when rapid change fails to do justice to past commitments and skills and (2) to point up the kinds of things an organization must do to change and develop new distinctive competencies.

An organization's character, then, consists of the ideas, beliefs, and hopes of people both inside and outside the organization about the appropriate role for the organization and about the way it will fulfill that role. It also consists of the skills, habits, and personal commitments of both insiders and outsiders that make the fulfillment of these role expectations possible.

Why a Book on Corporate Character?

Those of us who have written about corporate culture and culture change have often neglected the critical role of organizational skills as part of the culture and as a significant competitive advantage or disadvantage. Current work on corporate strategy stresses the critical importance of distinctive skills (Porter, 1987). However, few theorists in the area of strategy write about what such corporate skill consists of and how it is developed. That is a primary focus of *Developing Corporate Character.*

Discussion about culture change—both in writing and in the talk I hear among managers faced with this kind of change— too often centers around the future and around charismatic leadership. We seem to believe that charismatic leaders who can envision the future and passionately lead us there provide the solution to our problems. But our problems include dealing with the past. We must learn to honor the past commitments and skills of the firm and to encourage faith in the fairness of the organization if we want people to help implement new futures.

And we need leaders at many levels of the organization, not just at the top. I call these people "border guards," people at the boundaries of two or more subcultures who help manage the traffic between the subcultures. We need border guards who can protect subgroups in organizations long enough for the groups to develop new skills while at the same time helping them to understand and relate to the outside culture(s). Top management needs the help of these influential and knowledgeable people in the organization so they can understand existing skill while developing new skills and negotiating new visions. I argue that border guards in the middle of organizations often have more to do with the development of distinctive skills than the chief executive officer and others at the top.

In addition, we have tended to talk only about how to

start change and not how to carry it through the difficult implementation and ongoing development stages. I take a life cycle view of the development and adaptation of corporate character in this book. I discuss how to get started with change but also how to develop distinctive character for the long run and how to maintain and adapt it in the face of new challenges.

Many books written about major changes in organizations have focused on the positive, on examples of success. I think it is important to highlight success and to encourage others to try challenging tasks. However, I have spoken to so many managers who have failed at their attempts to create distinctive new organizational skills that I believe we must also understand and know how to avoid common mistakes. I have therefore included several examples of the struggles, failures, and mistakes involved in changing organizations. My hope is to encourage managers by helping them avoid the traps rather than discourage them because the task seems so daunting.

Who Should Read This Book?

I believe this book is particularly relevant to the following people:

- Senior executives, particularly those who face the need to make significant organizational changes. In addition, those senior executives whose firms have done well for many years may find instructive what I have written about how distinctive character can erode and be lost.
- "Border guards" in organizations—anyone who can carve out some space in the organization to create a subgroup character that is distinctive and who can help those in and out of the group to find faith and hope for the future, if only in a part of the organization.
- Those who help senior executives and more influential border guards: personnel or human resources people, consultants, and those in corporate strategy positions.
- Students of organizations. I hope that my academic colleagues will be interested in my efforts to expand and apply

the work of Selznick (1957) on distinctive competence and organizational character. I believe that students and professors who teach in professional schools will find these concepts useful in thinking about organizations.

- A broader audience of those interested in the progress of American business. My hope is that the concepts I have tried to develop and illustrate in *Developing Corporate Character* will be useful to those trying to understand the American business scene of the 1980s. I think that my view of organizational character and how it has been destroyed in some companies and developed in others provides insight into the history-making changes in our organizations.

Overview of the Contents

Chapter One presents an assessment of what happened on our way to excellence. I have observed over twenty organizations that have attempted significant change they would describe as culture change. A majority of these organizations have, from management's viewpoint, failed to achieve their objectives. I examine the failures and compare them briefly to the successes. I discuss the components of corporate character and how they can be destroyed or enhanced through change.

Part One discusses how to initiate significant change without destroying the character of the organization. Chapter Two defines and illustrates the components of corporate character that contribute to a distinctive competence. In this chapter I also offer questions that managers and others might use to assess their own corporate character. (The resource goes into much greater detail about how to assess the character of an organization.)

In Chapter Three I offer examples that show how an organization can change while honoring the past. The problem that organizations must resolve is how to convince people that the old ways do not work without destroying their faith both in the organization and in their personal ability to carry out the change. In addition, major change can make people fearful that they may not be treated fairly or given enough time to change. If these concerns are not addressed, most people resist change. I show that organizations can address these problems of employee expectations by honoring the past. Honoring the past includes acknowledging past mistakes and improving relationships as well as using the past for inspiration and instruction about how to change. It also provides direction so that organizations can begin to grow in new ways rather than forcing change that is inappropriate.

Part Two focuses on the problems of developing and embodying a shared vision. In Chapter Four I show that the problem for organizations engaged in change is not only to reassure employees about the fairness of the organization and its ability to adapt but also to develop shared ideas about the direction of changes. Since organizations develop subgroups with different orientations and beliefs about what the organization should do, developing a shared vision usually requires a somewhat political and incremental negotiation of various views. It includes experimenting with a variety of new skills and ideas and then jointly deciding what the results of these efforts suggest for new directions. I describe helpful visions and suggest ways that executives and managers can facilitate the development of a shared vision that is more than the rhetoric in a corporate mission statement.

Chapter Five describes the management actions that help to implement a shared vision. I describe the successful efforts of several executives and managers who helped their organizations develop new skills clearly related to a shared vision. I show that developing new corporate skills requires managing mistake making, encouraging the development of symbols, and developing supporting systems, structures, and policies.

Chapter Six is my effort to speak directly to those in the middle, the "border guards." I argue that border guards are more able to influence the development of real skills in the organization than anyone else, including the chief executive officer. I show what it means to create a subunit that has a distinctive character. I suggest the pitfalls and problems as well as the joys and achievements that accompany such efforts. I conclude the chapter with suggestions on how to manage the political and cultural problems associated with border guarding.

Part Three discusses the tensions involved in perpetuating a corporate character that must remain adaptive. Chapter Seven shows the necessity of protecting and perpetuating distinctive character. I offer a number of signs that reflect the erosion of corporate character and suggest means to halt that process.

Chapter Eight shows how the successful perpetuation of character often leads to organizational rigidity. I discuss the most common causes of rigidity, which all stem from somewhat normal responses to past successes. I then suggest ways to overcome some of the rigidity. I end the chapter with a discussion of the necessary tension that exists between maintaining critical traditions and continually changing and adapting.

Chapter Nine summarizes the book and delivers my challenge to all involved in organizations: we must be able to change organizations without destroying their character.

The resource helps practicing managers—or those who consult with them—determine the character of an organization. I describe the problems that must be overcome in order to understand corporate character and suggest ways to organize an assessment team, to design an assessment process, and to conduct interviews and other assessment activities. The goal of the assessment is to improve the organization's character in order to meet competitive challenges.

Acknowledgments

A book is always the end product of a network of people. I am finally responsible for what ends up on the printed page, but I would have been unable to develop and articulate these ideas without the insights, criticism, and encouragement of many people.

I owe a deep intellectual and personal debt to William Ouchi. His own work stimulated me to think about the character of social entities, and he supported my early efforts to study stories as remembered history and as a souce of organizational identity.

Gene Dalton has provided consistent encouragement, constructive criticism, and continual colleagueship, for which I will be ever grateful. He has not only written about mentorship but has served as a very effective mentor to me.

Many other colleagues have helped me with constructive comments: W. Gibb Dyer, Jr., Reba Keele, Kate Kirkham, Bonner Ritchie, and Keith Warner.

I am also grateful to administrators at Brigham Young University. Paul Thompson, dean of the School of Management, and Bonner Ritchie, department chair of Organizational Behavior, have been understanding and generous in helping me to find time and resources to work on this project.

Several generations of students in classes have helped me refine my ideas. In particular, Daken Tanner and Robin Zenger Baker have helped with research that led to many of the examples in the book. Nigel Bristow assisted in the research on negotiating a shared vision for Chapter Four. William Hesterly made very helpful suggestions on earlier drafts.

Many practitioners have also responded to my writing. Particularly helpful were Kim Fisher, Tektronix; Charles Feld, Frito-Lay; Michael Prior, formerly of Shell, Canada; Norman Smallwood and Jon Younger, Novations Group, Inc.; and Raymond Price, Boeing Commercial Airplane.

I also want to express gratitude for the opportunity to observe the management skills of several executives, who have served as inspirations for much of what I have written. Charles Feld at Frito-Lay has taught me more than I can say. Joel Peterson and Donald Williams at Trammell Crow, David Evans and Rodney Rougelot at Evans and Sutherland, and Gil Amelio, Richard Feller, and Randy Stott at Rockwell International have all been sources of great inspiration for me.

In addition, hundreds of executives and managers in programs for Covey and Associates have given me the benefit of their reactions and experiences. I am grateful to Stephen Covey and Ronald McMillan in particular for their thoughtful comments and for opportunities to try my ideas with different audiences. I am also grateful for their example of moral integrity.

Kerry Patterson, Francis Price, and David Maxfield, all of Interact Performance Systems, have provided rich opportunities to learn from joint consulting projects. In particular, I want to thank Kerry Patterson for his colleagueship, his insightful comments on my ideas, and his friendship.

Most of all, I am grateful to my wife, Margaret, and our seven children, whose patience with me during the birthing pains of this book made it possible. They have inspired my concern for long-term ties that both bind and free us and that allow us to be the best we can be.

Provo, Utah   Alan L. Wilkins
November 1988

The Author

Alan L. Wilkins is professor of organizational behavior in the Graduate School of Management of Brigham Young University. He received his B.A. degree (1972) in Spanish and his M.B.A. degree (1974) from Brigham Young University. His Ph.D. degree (1979) in organizational behavior is from Stanford University.

Wilkins's major research activities have focused on organizational culture and culture change. He has studied the role of informally told stories in passing on management philosophy and culture. He has also investigated the ways in which culture change efforts fail. He has written numerous articles on these subjects for both academic and practitioner audiences. His articles have appeared in the *Administrative Science Quarterly*, the *Annual Review of Sociology*, *Organizational Dynamics*, *Human Resource Management*, and the *Academy of Management Review*, as well as in several other journals and in several edited books.

Wilkins has been quoted as an expert on culture and stories in *The Wall Street Journal*, *Fortune*, and *Dunn's Review*. He has also addressed numerous management audiences and consulted with a number of organizations. Consulting clients include Hewlett-Packard, Ford Motor Company, Frito-Lay, Rockwell, American Express, Trammell Crow, and Tektronix, as well as other organizations in industries such as health care and public utilities.

Developing
Corporate Character

1

What Happened on the Way to Excellence?

Recently, the chief executive officer (CEO) of a medium-sized company asked me to help him "install a new culture." Not long after that, a colleague of mine reported that following one of his more impassioned presentations on excellent companies another CEO turned to his subordinates and demanded: "I want one of those excellent company cultures and Monday would not be too soon!"

Of course, the implications of these requests—that changing corporate culture is like installing a new cooling system or that it can be achieved by fiat—are ludicrous. Indeed, most managers I talk with display significantly greater sophistication. Unfortunately, some of them have learned the hard way how difficult it is to "manage culture."

The past decade has seen a dramatic increase in the number of executives who claim that they are "changing the culture" of their companies. And why not? Myriad external changes have combined to make executives reconsider the very nature of their organizations. Many companies have faced simultaneously such formidable challenges as dramatically improved foreign competition, deregulation, and rapidly changing technology, as well as significant new trends in our domestic culture such as those John Naisbitt highlighted in his book *Megatrends* (1984).

1

No wonder *Theory Z* (Ouchi, 1981), *In Search of Excellence* (Peters and Waterman, 1982), and *A Passion for Excellence* (Peters and Austin, 1985) became best-sellers. They promised, by implication, that if the bulk of America's companies would imitate the practices of certain successful firms, they too would be much more successful. Some managers intentionally attempted to imitate these practices while others have employed alternative models. Whatever the ideal was, many businesses have failed to change as much as they wanted, and they often encountered significant problems as they engaged in dramatic organizational transitions. In their rush to become more competitive, they have often destroyed some intangibles that are the essence of what makes an organization competitive in the long run. Consider the following example.

Culture Change Can Destroy Character

Over the past several years, I have followed the progress of a previously regulated utility company that is an excellent, if distressing, example of what is lost when executives do not manage change well. The company was forced to make dramatic changes following government deregulation. The company had a venerated tradition of thoughtful, cooperative management and reliable customer service, but its executives decided to encourage a complete overhaul in the way they did business. First among these changes was the desire to become competitive and to develop new products for an unregulated marketplace. They now operate with cutthroat competitive vigor, competing not only with other companies but also with other parts of their own company. Morale is very low, and the company has failed in many ventures, often because managers do not coordinate their efforts or share information with one another.

This company was previously an example of management effectiveness. It was one of the highest performing companies in its industry. What had been lost? I cannot think of a better example of a company that has lost its sense of identity—lost its character, its soul. Clearly, managers in the company do not "know who they are." Indeed, the company has lost three critical and often intangible components of what it means to have an organizational character.

Components of Organizational Character

Shared Vision
> A common understanding of organizational purpose and identity; a sense of "who we are"

Motivational Faith
> - In *fairness* (of the leaders and of others)
> - In *ability* (personal and organizational)

Distinctive Skills
> The tacit customs, the networks of experts, and the technology that add up to collective organizational competence

To a large extent, this company has lost its shared vision, motivational faith, and distinctive skills. It has clearly lost a shared understanding of organizational purpose. Previously, many employees had taken great pride in the service that they performed for the community. Now many are cynical about the "money grubbing" and "selfishness" that seem to be the firm's motives. Whereas the company once had an excellent reputation among customers and in the community, its inability to meet new commitments has led to a significantly tarnished image. For these reasons, employees are no longer as proud to be part of this organization and no longer have a clear sense of what this organization is supposed to do.

Perhaps even more critically, many employees have lost the motivation that once fueled their individual contributions. Specifically, they have lost a motivational hope for appropriate rewards and success. This hope comes in part from a faith in the fairness of the organization, its leaders, and other employees. It also stems from confidence that "I can contribute and will therefore be rewarded and accepted for my efforts" (Ouchi, 1980; Wilkins and Ouchi, 1983). Many employees previously had implicit faith that if they devoted themselves to working hard and developing appropriate skills, then they would be rewarded. They believed that their sacrifices to make the organization succeed would be noticed and at least remembered. Given the current drastic changes, they are no longer sure. From their point of view, they are making great sacrifices, and yet their efforts are never good enough. They seem to be rewarded only with criticism within the company. They have also lost their faith in the broader organization and its abilities. Therefore, they are less willing to stay with the company and to try to make sure that it works.

Faith motivates and shared purpose guides employees' efforts. The loss of these two components of organizational character significantly decreased the performance of this company. People were simply less willing to put in the effort they did previously. They lacked faith that their efforts would be rewarded, and without a shared purpose, they were not sure what to do in any case.

The third component of corporate character that has been lost is the organization's skill. People did not suddenly lose ability as individuals, but when the organization abandoned its distinctive habits, customs, and skills, employees no longer saw how to apply their talents. Many employees have concluded that they do not know how to do anything. By their feedback and their desire to change everything, executives imply that none of the old skills is particularly helpful. In addition, the new competitiveness between organizational subunits and lack of trust in the fairness of leaders have significantly reduced the cooperation among networks of experts that previously contributed to the organization's distinctive skills.

Avoid Losing Character: Honor Your Past

An important moral from the experience of this utility company is that leaders contemplating the need for significant changes should look first to what they want to keep. They should consider the costs of directly attacking current traditions and competence. And if they decide that dramatic changes are necessary, they must plan for and be willing to work through the inevitable inefficiency that accompanies the creation of new organizational purposes and skills.

This sensitivity to past commitments, past skills, and past purposes is what I call "honoring the past." The point is not that we should cling to the past. Rather, we must recognize what makes up a distinctive organizational character and realize how difficult it is to develop and how easily it can be lost.

Those who led change in the utility company overlooked many opportunities to show how old skills could be applied to new problems. They failed to identify the purposes and values from the past that would continue. Most importantly, they did not help individuals who had spent careers trying to embody certain values and skills have faith that they would be given a fair chance at change.

Indeed, the most critical component of character to maintain and the easiest to lose is faith. If employees lose their sense that the organization will be fair and that their sacrifices to develop new skills will be rewarded, then they are unlikely to make committed, joint efforts to develop a new concept of the business. They are also unlikely to stay around long enough or make great enough efforts to learn new and distinctive skills.

An organization can be relatively incompetent for some time if its people believe that eventually they will develop new competence and will become competitive and see the rewards of their efforts. Similarly, people can accept a loss of clarity about the purpose of the business if they believe that their efforts to develop a new concept of the business will be rewarded.

Hence, the most crucial component of character when we talk of change is the motivation that comes from faith in the fairness of the organization and its ability to change. Unfortunately, these are the very beliefs executives destroy first when they try to motivate people to change by showing them the inadequacies of the old system. They must help employees maintain or develop faith and hope at the same time that they raise questions about former purposes and skills. Managing this tension to create and develop distinctive corporate character is the subject of this book. Managing this tension well is the essence of leadership in situations of change.

Consider an illustration of this kind of leadership in action. Executives in the company I will describe understood that paradoxically an organization can change much faster, and arrive at a new distinctive competence much more quickly, if managers take time to honor past commitments and competencies. In this sense, slow is fast.

The company is Stop and Shop, a retail firm. It has been successful for decades and prides itself on its ability to adapt quickly. Some members of this organization believe that they learned from a series of events in the 1960s that they could make significant changes without losing essential aspects of their character.

In the sixties, many Americans moved to the suburbs, and most retail outlets that remained viable had to move with them. As Stop and Shop built stores in suburban locations, executives soon discovered that its division general managers were much too autocratic and operated with too much centralization. They learned that operating far-flung and decentralized operations in a variety of suburbs required less centralized pricing and buying. However, division general managers remained centralized and autocratic. They thwarted efforts to allow differences among stores in their divisions.

Executives of the firm conducted an informal survey and discovered that at least 65 or 70 percent of Stop and Shop's managers had inappropriate management styles for the new operations that the executives envisioned. Some executives called for a purge of the most recalcitrant managers to speed up the change. Instead, the president insisted that the managers be given an opportunity to change. The leadership made it clear that these managers were valued and still had many useful skills. They also conducted training programs in which they described very clearly the necessary new style and the reasons for the changes. They asked old-style managers to visit and observe successful managers. The company spent two to three years trying to develop the new skills, values, and relationships that were critical for success.

A number of the division general managers decided to leave the firm, and others decided to move to other positions within the firm. But the vast majority of the division general managers changed significantly. Certainly, some changed more than others, but overall change was significant and visible.

The moral of this history for Stop and Shop managers is that their company is fair. The change was successful because executives reassured people about their ability and the fairness of the company, while they encouraged employees to understand the new concept of the business and to develop new skills. As a result, these managers have become convinced not only that they have distinctive skills for running decentralized operations but also that they know how to change. People change more quickly when they feel they will be treated fairly and given the opportunity to contribute to, and be rewarded for, the changes. In other words, slow is fast works for current changes, as well as for later ones, because people will be more ready to change quickly when they have confidence in their ability to adapt. A critical component of this confidence is faith in the fairness of the organization during change attempts.

How Attempts to Change Culture Can Destroy Character

For the past seven years, I have gathered information on companies that have been attempting self-proclaimed "culture" change. What troubles me is how often attempts to change culture destroy organizational character. I hope that understanding the most common ways organizations fail in changing culture will help others avoid these mistakes. In the following pages I describe developing corporate character as an alternative to these typical attempts to change culture. My sample now includes twenty-two organizations, both large and small; half of them are *Fortune* 500 size. They also represent organizations in several different industries. Of the twenty-two organizations in my sample, nine were long-term consulting clients. I have gathered information from four companies through in-depth interviews with those who were either facilitating the change or were managing the company. Three of the companies are so prominent in the popular press that I have been able to construct from accounts in the business press, occasionally supplemented by business school cases, rich, though incomplete, descriptions of efforts in these companies. I studied the final six companies by using historical and qualitative research methods.

Managers in at least sixteen of these twenty-two organi-

zations would label their attempts at major change a failure.
That is, they have not achieved their own objectives, and in
many cases their efforts have created serious cynicism among
employees because the company was unable to change as promised. Two of the companies are not clearly a success or failure,
while executives in the remaining four organizations feel they
have mainly succeeded in making dramatic changes.

I believe that these failures to change all stem from trying
to take shortcuts to obtain new skills. I believe there are no
shortcuts. What fascinates me is that there are some common
reasons these companies fail when attempting significant change.
They include (1) piecemeal imitation of successful organizations,
(2) attempts to import a new culture, and (3) fostering organizational revolution. Let us consider these three reasons for failure.

Piecemeal Imitation of Successful Organizations. Several
of the companies in my sample tried to implement generally
praiseworthy ideas or practices from successful companies, but
the result was typically cynicism rather than hoped-for productivity improvements. For example, quality circles, statistical
process control, and just-in-time inventory reduction techniques
were some of the borrowed practices. Such new programs may
fail to meet expectations for many reasons: the programs require new skills, they do not fit the local conditions in different
subunits, they are not reinforced by organizational rewards,
they threaten to give some people less influence, or they receive
only lip service from management. But most of these reasons
can be subsumed under a general one: Programs work in one
setting because of a mix of personalities, specific historical conditions, widely shared values, organizational skills, and supporting systems. When they are wrenched from these contextual
supports, there is no guarantee they will work in a new context.

The president of a medical instruments firm illustrates
the most obvious form of imitation. His employees believe that
he introduces "a new program every two months." They concluded cynically that if they read the *Harvard Business Review*,
they could predict his next new formula, theme, or program.
And they responded in general by enduring the onslaught of

new programs and assuming that none would stay very long. Hence, the organization became immune to almost anything introduced.

The managers of a Canadian company read *Theory Z* and decided that they should produce a management philosophy statement that encouraged teamwork throughout the organization. Their document promised that the company would protect and develop employees and asked for employee loyalty in return. The company would avoid layoffs at all cost, would seek to train and develop employees, and, in return, would expect that employees would be productive and participate in helping to solve the firm's problems.

Unfortunately, within two years of this statement of management philosophy, the company experienced a serious business downturn and executives felt forced to lay off approximately 30 percent of its employees. In addition, several groups within the firm interpreted the management philosophy statement to be an endorsement of their own efforts to develop managers. When company officials rebuffed every proposal these groups made to establish management development programs, they felt company officials had reneged on their promises. The resulting cynicism about corporate management in this company has made improvements in performance almost impossible.

Marvin Bowers, the legendary founder of McKinsey and Company, once suggested that programs and information developed to work within a particular organization would rarely work the same way, if at all, in another. Speaking initially of advertising agencies, he said:

> If a company rests its policy of not letting its agencies serve competitors on the need for security of information, it does not have a very solid base. As a matter of realism, the interests of competing clients would not be harmed by an almost complete exchange of information among people serving the two competing companies. Of course, no responsible service firm would do that—and indeed they go

to great lengths to avoid even inadvertent exchanges. Nevertheless, as one who has been a repos-
itory of confidential information over many years,
I am convinced that the history, makeup, ways of
doing business, attitudes of people, operating philosophy and procedures of even directly competing
companies are ordinarily so different that information could be exchanged between them with no
harm to either [Ogilvy, 1983, p. 69].

Distinctive organizational performance is mostly the result of deeply ingrained repertoires developed over time. Adopt-
ing a program or practice from another firm is likely to require
more than just an understanding of procedures or a particular
technology.

Economists have called this problem "imperfect imitability" (Lippman and Rumelt, 1982; Barney, 1986). In essence,
the problem is that firms in one industry are not likely to know
specifically what makes some other firms successful, so they do
not know what to imitate. However, even if they had a good
idea about the complex of things a successful firm does, they
would still be unable to quickly or accurately imitate those
things because much of the successful firm's knowledge or skill
is tacit and therefore partially taken for granted even by people
in the successful firm. As Nelson and Winters (1982) argue, the
skills and knowledge of firms are located in the habits, memories, skills, and commitments of groups of their employees. An
individual practices or understands only part of any organizational skill. Skills become organizational as individuals combine
their efforts.

A myth among many executives is that they can implement the practices of successful companies and reap their success. Sustainable competitive advantage, however, comes only
from developing unique social conventions, skills, and orientations within the firm.

LaVell Edwards, the coach of Brigham Young University's 1984 national championship football team, calls this competitive advantage "execution." He has said that he could give

opponents the playbook and even his game plan and they would still be unable to stop his offense if his team executes well. Execution comes from disciplined practice, from each person doing his part and helping out as the play develops and as players have to adjust. Players come to know what to expect from each other and can therefore adapt to each other rapidly when exceptions occur.

You cannot copy execution; you have to develop it through trial and error with motivated employees willing to make personal sacrifices and adjustments to achieve something distinctive. If this were not so, then no company should be interested in developing a distinctive organizational culture. That is, if it were easy to imitate the culture of IBM or of Procter & Gamble, then these firms would not have a competitive advantage. What they have developed in the way of a unique culture is a competitive advantage precisely because it is the product of years of careful building.

Lest anyone imagine that I would advise executives not to borrow ideas from successful companies, let me clarify. My real concern is that executives will borrow with the expectation of a quick fix (Kilmann, 1984). They then behave like the president of the medical instruments firm described earlier and forever introduce new programs. They fail to give employees enough time to adapt the practices to the firm's particular needs and to develop the skills and insights to execute them well. As a result, new programs frequently threaten employees and managers who resist them with good reason.

Perhaps the greatest genius of the Japanese is demonstrated by their tenacity in learning what our companies have done and then adapting our practices to fit their style. They make an art out of insisting on execution. They did not invent quality circles, or statistical process control, or just-in-time inventory reduction techniques, but they tend to adapt and execute them better than American firms do. For example, a recent summary of research on quality circles in the United States suggests that most companies experience an initial excitement about the early quality circle groups but that they falter in implementing the program throughout the company. Managers eventually stop paying close attention to the groups once the pilot testing is over. Subsequently, the training and the time off work required to support the expansion of quality circles throughout the organization lead many managers to question and disband the groups before they have much impact (Lawler and Mohrman, 1987).

Charles Feld, vice president of management services at Frito-Lay, provides an excellent example of *adapting* rather than imitating. His group is one of the most enthusiastic and highest performing groups at Frito-Lay. In 1981, when he took over the group, it was troubled by 38 percent turnover, low competence, and a poor reputation in the company. He personally interviewed employees and determined the group's needs, values, and skills, even though he hired several consultants to help in the diagnosis.

In addition to adding some new technical systems, Feld recognized that many of the improvements he wanted to foster were represented in a program of videotapes developed by Zenger-Miller and Thomas Peters to explain how firms can develop excellent company characteristics. However, as he thoughtfully reviewed the material, he could see that several ideas did not fit. For instance, the ideas about a "bias to action" ("ready, fire, aim") did not particularly fit the task of his group, which develops the complex and integrated computer systems on which everyone at Frito-Lay depends. Planning and developing consensus before taking action are critical for his group.

Feld also wanted employees to understand the particular character and needs of Frito-Lay rather than only the general ideas of the Zenger-Miller tapes. He used the tapes as a broad introduction to ideas and then discussed the specific needs of Frito-Lay in each of many sessions for several levels in his organization. He then spent a few hours in each session leading a discussion about how to apply the ideas and how to modify some of them. He also encouraged people to experiment with applying the ideas and to learn from and share both their successes and failures with others. Feld has emphasized these ideas consistently in meetings and encouraged various groups of managers to come up with ideas for application and suggestions for improvement for several years.

The result? Turnover is down to 10 percent, the division has handled a record number of systems development projects, and even under increased performance expectations, it recently scored the highest satisfaction ratings of the entire organization.

Feld did not just adopt a program. He was thoughtful about using what he could find that fit with his perspective and then adapting what he found. He was willing to direct the initial diagnosis, training, and subsequent learning necessary to develop the execution insights and skills that made the program successful.

Unless managers are willing to adapt borrowed ideas and programs and struggle through the development of execution skills, they will see little improvement from applying the latest programs. Many of the programs will simply be inappropriate. But even the appropriate ones will often fail to produce results. Indeed, the most frequent result of the expectation that companies can make significant changes rapidly is cynicism. Employees come to realize that even when managers seem to be sincere and have taken time to think about the new changes, their announcement of change is rarely followed up with change in the way things really work.

Attempts to Import a New Culture. Recently, executives in a previously very successful pharmaceutical firm decided that their marketing prowess needed to be buttressed with the ability to develop new products. They soon acquired a research group of forty people. The group had developed several very creative products as an independent laboratory, and executives were delighted at the prospects of merging this research and development skill with their own marketing orientation. The firm quickly imposed its brief product development time frames and specific market constraints on the R&D group. The result was high turnover in the R&D group and very little help with new products.

This pharmaceutical firm had been successful in executing a competitive marketing orientation because it was able to identify and meet specific market needs rapidly. That was why it had been unable to allow the loose structure, longer time frames, and unpredictable hit rates that characterized the R&D

group and had contributed to its success. Hence, the hoped-for synergy became almost impossible to obtain without destroying a significant element in either the firm or the R&D group. By emphasizing the marketing orientation, the firm destroyed the feeling in the R&D group that it was valued and would be treated fairly. Creating synergy would have required negotiating a credible new vision for both sides and reassuring both that their competence would be needed and their best interests protected. In addition, the firm would have needed to develop joint skills that integrated both R&D and marketing competencies.

Some firms have tried a variant of importing a new culture. They attempt to buy a high-performing firm and let it operate on its own. The major problem with this strategy is that usually the acquiring firm will have to pay the full market value for the purchased firm. That is, to the extent that a competitive market is operating, the price for the acquired firm will be the discounted value of expected future earnings. If the acquired firm is performing well, then the buyer will pay enough for it that any future earnings will not give much of a return on the buyer's investment.

In a recent *Harvard Business Review* article, Michael Porter (1987) claims that acquiring firms that do not add value to the new firm have low returns. Unless there is synergy between the two firms that continues to produce and improve on the acquired firm's distinctive competence, the acquiring firm will not reap benefits. Some firms have been able to acquire a firm, add some new competence to it in a few years, and then sell the firm for a profit. In such instances, however, the acquiring firm must have a developed talent for passing on competence and must devote the patience and attention of key executives to this task. Executives must also discipline themselves to continue to add value or to sell the acquired firm and start over before the value of newly passed on skills is lost when competitors develop similar skills.

In related research, Richard Rumelt (1974) found that firms were most successful over a long time when they followed a strategy of "related diversification." Firms that did not diversify at all apparently did not adapt enough to new conditions to perform well in the long run. And firms that became conglomerates were apparently unable to apply a central skill and add value to very diverse acquired firms. When the "related diversifiers" applied an appropriate central skill to different competitive arenas rather than trying to adopt completely different skills (typically through acquisition), they were more competitive.

The problem is the same when we turn our focus away from companies to individuals. Many firms assume that hiring an executive from an "excellent company" will help bring some of that company's magic into their own firm. Indeed, for five years now I have watched executives in a high-tech computer firm try to hire management talent to help them cope with the significant growth of the firm. The firm has been managed by a Ph.D. scientist who fostered state-of-the-art developments and a strong technical orientation that have brought the company its growth. The president recognized the need for marketing, finance, accounting, and other skills that the company has not developed to the point of sophistication. Over several years he hired executives from successful and larger firms to become vice presidents. In almost every case (five out of seven), the new executives were fired in less than a year. In each instance, the new executive brought expectations for new systems and control without a sensitivity to the company's history and technical expertise. He would invariably threaten the creativity and flexibility in the firm that had led to its significant innovations.

From the examination of these first two reasons for failure in changing culture, the conclusion is inescapable. Organizational skill that has competitive value takes time to develop whether you try to imitate the know-how or to import it in the form of a new firm or new people. The problem is not that firms cannot learn from each other but rather that the learning is imperfect, takes time, and must be adapted to the ongoing orientations, routines, and skills of the firm. The new know-how requires execution skills, and execution skills are developed through practice and consistent nurturing. It also has to be adapted to a new organizational context in which people have developed alternative skills and orientations and may thus feel threatened. You cannot buy a distinctive organizational culture and you cannot copy it from someone else. You must grow it.

Essentially, we have been considering efforts to change a firm's culture by importing either ideas and practices or people from other firms. When ideas or practices are imported, the people implementing them potentially understand the current context but do not understand the nuances of the idea or have execution skills. When people (individuals or a whole organization) are imported, the new people may understand the new competence, but they lack the relationships and integration skills to make sure that competence fits and develops synergy with the existing competence in the new organizational context. Apparently, you simply cannot have your cake and eat it too.

Let us now turn to a different kind of problem in culture change: how change is attempted. Having discussed the problems of importing ideas, practices, or people, let us look at problems that occur because executives feel desperate or lose control and the organization goes through a revolution that may include bringing in ideas, practices, and people simultaneously and abruptly.

Changing the Culture Through Revolution. After presenting in-depth historical studies of six companies, W. Gibb Dyer, Jr. (1985), summarized the typical process he saw when firms achieved observable cultural change. The process, best characterized as revolutionary, consists of the following steps: (1) the methods and orientations that the "old guard" sponsors are questioned because of a perceived crisis in the firm's performance, (2) the old leaders are replaced by new executives, (3) the new executives introduce new methods and orientations, (4) the firm's performance improves and employees attribute this to the new methods, and (5) the new leadership institutionalizes the new methods through its own reward systems, organizational structure, and hiring patterns. Dyer claims that when these conditions are not fully met, cultural change does not occur. The attempted changes are eventually undone.

If revolution works, then why not use it? The problem with using revolution as a change strategy is that revolution is very difficult to control. Indeed, the implication for managers is that unless they are the new leaders, revolution is not likely to help their personal cause. In addition, my observations of several efforts to change cultures suggest at least four ways that firms can fail if they use revolution to change:

1. Absence of a shared perception of crisis: Employees do not band together because they still think the old ways are fine, the problem is not severe, or old change strategies will solve the problem. They may resist believing in a crisis because that would threaten their influence and confidence.
2. No clear alternative is available: People debate what new ideas, practices, and values to implement. They do not understand or are not able to implement the new ways.
3. Performance does not improve: Results are no better with the new ideas, practices, and values. They are often questioned just as the old ways were.
4. People learn the wrong lessons: Rather than learning new ways, employees may learn how to successfully resist changes while appearing to support them.

   1. *Absence of a shared perception of crisis:* The performance indicators in a major construction firm for some time had suggested to the board of directors that the firm was in serious trouble. However, the firm was composed of several previously separate construction companies; some were not performing as poorly as others. When the board of directors replaced the president who had grown up in the business with an outside professional manager, several local managers resisted the new president's efforts to change. The previous orientation favored local control, so regional or local managers saw new centralized controls from headquarters as a serious threat. In addition, local managers lacked the full array of financial indicators; each manager only knew of his local concerns and did not see them as concerns that others in the firm necessarily shared. These regional managers gave the impression in corporate meetings that they supported the new leadership, but they would subsequently undermine the new senior leadership as they

worked with their own people in regional settings. It soon became clear to a coalition of regional managers, many of whom had connections with the board of directors, that the new senior leadership was the real source of crisis rather than their own regional ineptness.

The new professional manager lasted only a year in the company. His replacement was selected from among the regional managers, and it is not yet clear whether this new manager can create enough consensus about the problems confronting the firm to take focused and effective action.

2. *No clear alternative available:* Warner Woodworth and Chris Meek (1984) have written about their long-term experience with employee ownership at Rath Meat Packing and at Hyatt Clark Industries. Following a serious economic crisis at both of these companies, employees purchased stock and became the majority owners. The new structure in each firm involved having employees on the board of directors. In essence, the supervisors and managers of the firm were reporting to their subordinates. These companies had few precedents to draw on. The new situation has made it very difficult for employees and managers to understand how to operate in this ownership and management structure. In each case, management has developed its own union and now has its own representatives to bargain with its employees, the owners. Apparently, the only way these groups of managers and employees know how to relate is through the adversarial means familiar to them.

Hence, even though a group may share a definition of the problem, if the alternative to be implemented is not clearly worked out, then the result may be a return to former cultural patterns or significant confusion.

3. *Performance does not improve:* The problem here is to get participants to perceive that the new methods and the new orientation are somehow producing improvement. However, if performance fails to improve after some time, or deteriorates, then the new alternative is often rejected. A well-known example of just such a failure comes from Roy Ash in his tenure at Addressograph-Multigraph. He had plans for making the company the next IBM. He changed the name of the company to

AM International and replaced much of the company's management with his own people. He moved company headquarters from Cleveland to Los Angeles. He acquired several high-tech companies and captivated Wall Street investors with his vision of the future potential of AM International. Many believe that his vision of applying state-of-the-art electronics to aging electro-mechanical products was sound but poorly executed. In any case, in 1981 AM lost $245 million on $857 million in sales and soon after Ash was ousted. The company had to file for protection under Chapter 11 ("AM International . . . ," 1982).

4. *Employees learn the wrong lesson:* Few companies have been as badly battered by their own management as RCA. It has frequently been cited by the popular press as an example of inconsistency at the top over a decade. During that time, it has had no fewer than four different CEOs, each with an apparently different strategy. David Sarnoff, Sr., began with an effort to make the company technologically superior. His son, however, attempted to bring the company into a new era by buying many unrelated businesses, hoping that the firm would become better at marketing. He was succeeded by two presidents who sought in turn to first return the firm to its previous technological strength and then recently to slow down changes and just manage the status quo. During this period of constant change, the business press has reported the development of a series of fiefdoms, groups of people who have learned to survive by their wits. They are careful to appear to be supporting new directions. In reality, they follow their own lead, realizing that within a short period things will change again at the top. They learned to expect revolution, and therefore revolution changed very little (" 'RCA': Will It Ever . . . ," 1984). Revolution may thus produce significant organizational rigidity that leads to another revolution. The cycle is vicious at best.

Changing an organization's culture, even by revolution, is fraught with risks. Revolution, if it is successful, can change a company's culture. However, the change may destroy or inhibit the development of a distinctive corporate character. The culture may become so prone to revolution that it is ineffective.

Many cite Lee Iacocca as an example of someone who has

turned his company around and influenced its culture through revolution. What is clear in Iacocca's case is that he has stanched the flow of red ink. However, the company has survived by paring down to bare bones, producing only a few products, and it has yet to develop a major competitive strength against Japanese or other American automobile companies. It takes some time to develop the new skills and new habits that make a new orientation efficient even when the initial revolution is successful.

Often executives may feel that they do not have enough time for patient development of new execution skills, so they must therefore turn to the abrupt and drastic changes that I have called revolution. I suggest a warning: Revolutions often successfully destroy many aspects of the past without giving people something new to work with. Tragically, most companies that go through revolutions in leadership, in style, and in the markets they address are left without helpful precedents—without a usable past. Creating an entirely new history will, of necessity, take time. There is no alternative. And if the past skills and the faith employees have in the fairness and ability of the company are lost, the new history may not be very exciting.

Developing Organizational Character:
The Leadership Challenge

The inescapable conclusion from both the research cited and these observations is that those who would change organizations must honor the past. They must begin by encouraging faith in the fairness of the organization and the ability of its people to make change. They must help people move from past purposes and skills to new ones. Change will require that managers have patience and that they "muddle through" a variety of experiences in which they learn, experiment, and make mistakes. Such skill-developing experiences will be necessary whether or not a firm acquires another organization or borrows new ideas and practices. Evolution rather than revolution is the way to change organizations if we want to develop a clear and distinctive corporate character as I have defined it.

From this point of view, all of the current talk about

transformational leadership seems both relevant and dangerous. Transformational leaders may indeed be necessary to help create new visions and overcome resistance to required changes. However, such leaders may look very much like Roy Ash, formerly of AM International. As my observations and Roy Ash's difficulties suggest, leaders must learn to buttress their visions of the future with deep appreciation for their organizations' past commitments, habits, and values. They must learn to start within that context and help participants bridge past and future. Unfortunately, in our current headlong rush into the future, we often take the past for granted.

The challenge for organizational leaders is enormous. Our times require change, often radical change. In most cases, only through great willpower will leaders be able to resist the pressures to move too fast. If organizational leaders fail to step forward and exercise remarkable personal character and insight, then the character of many of our greatest institutions could easily be lost.

2

Assess Corporate Character: Determining What to Keep and What to Change

By the late 1970s, *Business Week* hailed Precision Instruments (a pseudonym) as one of the five best growth companies in the United States. The company had developed a modular design for instruments that allowed significant cost advantages, great flexibility in customizing, and a significant competitive advantage.

Company executives felt they had treated their employees very well. For example, employees received profit sharing that could equal up to 10 percent of their yearly take-home pay. In addition, individual employees received bonuses of up to 25 percent of their salary if their contribution was exceptional. Whether they worked in engineering or manufacturing, employees took pride in the company's progress.

During its first ten years, Precision Instruments inhabited rather spartan quarters. For most of that period, the company was in cramped quarters in an abandoned drugstore warehouse. Managers shared secretaries, and production employees, engineers, and managers bumped into one another almost daily. Harold Phelps (all names are also pseudonyms), one of the three founders, also spent a lot of time with the manufacturing employees and developed a very good relationship with them.

The company's success allowed the founders to build a beautiful new office complex that provided significantly greater space. The mahogany paneling, thick carpets, and oak desks of the executive offices and the nine-hole golf course, hangar for the new company plane, and artificial lake (complete with ducks) all combined to say that the company had arrived. Employees willingly worked on their own time and used their own cars and trucks to help move the company into its new setting.

Imagine the surprise of the founders when, in the two years following the move, the company profits declined significantly; sales continued to increase, though not as much as in the past. As far as they could tell, the major problem was decreased productivity of the manufacturing employees. Indeed, many were calling for a union to represent their interests, and they had enough votes to call for an election. What happened?

My investigation suggested that the founders had inadvertently allowed employees to develop strong feelings that they were in the dark about a number of new challenges and changes. Apparently, the executive-founders became preoccupied with several different problems and were unaware of the erosion of their firm's unique character.

In the first place, Phelps, the founder most closely associated with the manufacturing employees, retired at the time of the move. The other two founders found themselves embroiled in a patent infringement lawsuit, which claimed that their new products used a patented process. The founders subsequently hired several design engineers and began to focus even more heavily on new product development, in part because they lost the patent infringement case.

To make matters worse, the new products were more specialized and harder to produce than were the old ones. Employees did not understand why they had more rework. Managers had not focused on developing new skills, and new suppliers were not providing the same quality of raw materials as older suppliers had, thus adding to rework. Managers unwisely pushed to shorten delivery times on new products, and when employees told them about quality problems in the materials, managers ordered employees to quit complaining and use what they had. The rework increased further.

Part of the pressure on management to push products out the door came from an economic downturn that depressed the entire industry. As a result, the company did not meet its expected sales goals during the first year after the move and was thus paying for considerable excess capacity. Precision Instruments did not meet its profit-sharing goal, and employees received no profit sharing the first year.

The building itself suggested a two-class system that was clearly different from employees' previous experience. Manufacturing employees were not allowed in the richly furnished area set aside for the executives for fear that the off-white carpet would get dirty.

No one dramatic change occurred. Instead, an accumulation of small messages indicated to many employees that the old order of things, where they felt involved in the company's progress and felt appreciated and rewarded for their involvement, had changed. When employees tried to share their concerns, the founders seemed to blame them for the troubles. The employees' response was to consider inviting a union in to represent them in bargaining with management.

Notice that the erosion of corporate character at Precision Instruments happened gradually and involved a complex intertwining of the components of character. Faith in the fairness and in the viability of the company eroded when employees were slow in developing new skills for working with new products. They were less willing to develop new skills because they were not sure they would be rewarded fairly and because they were unsure what skills and priorities were most important.

Figure 1 depicts this mutually reinforcing relationship among the components of corporate character.

Figure 1. Relationships of Character Components.

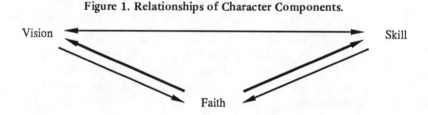

Faith provides the foundation. If people believe that they will be treated fairly and have confidence that the organization can become competent, then they are willing to cooperate on developing shared vision and appropriate execution skills. However, we can also see from the example of Precision Instruments that when vision and skills erode, faith is also affected. As the vision of employees lost its focus, they were no longer sure when and how to use their skills or what new skills to develop. Employees lost pride in their product and the confidence that had previously reinforced their faith in the organization. Without a shared clarity of priorities and confidence in their collective skills, how could they trust evaluations of their performance? How could they believe that the organization would continue to be successful enough to provide profit sharing or other rewards?

This chapter is devoted to showing managers what to look for in assessing their corporate character not just when they plan for change but also as changes occur. I will suggest what managers can look for to determine whether the components of corporate character are present or are eroding. Because the components of character are mutually reinforcing, and because erosion in one component can damage the others, I separate them only for convenience of exposition. We will consider each component of corporate character in turn.

Faith: The Foundation of Organizational Character

The key to the erosion of a unique organizational character at Precision Instruments was the loss of employee faith in the organization's fairness and viability. I call this most essential ingredient of corporate character "social capital." (Stephen Covey, 1987, has developed a similar concept, which he calls the "emotional bank account.") Like financial capital, social capital can be created, spent, and used up. It allows people in an organization to get things done, and not much can be accomplished without it. However, we might say that social capital is both an asset and a liability. It can be spent to encourage resilience when the organization faces complex and unexpected challenges. In-

deed, the faith that problems can and will be resolved often becomes a self-fulfilling prophecy. But if the social capital is
squandered, then employees tend to become more resistant and
self-protective than might be the case otherwise. Perhaps another
look at Precision Instruments will make this analogy clearer.

From the company's beginning, its founders were consistent and trustworthy in certain ways, and employees had come
to trust them. Employees did not expect to understand everything immediately, and the founders had considerable leeway to
try new things. In addition, employees felt motivated to give
their best effort and to make new practices or products work.

When things started to change, employees assumed they
could resolve problems. However, as we have seen, the founders
did not seem to understand the employees. Perhaps because
Harold Phelps was gone and because of their preoccupations,
they seemed to blame the changes on employee laziness.

Because employees initially had high expectations of fair
treatment and of being able to work out misunderstandings, it
took some time for many of them to lose hope. Indeed, many
still think that a "return to the old days" is possible. However,
for many, a comparison of the previously high levels of trust
with current operations shows how bad things have become.
These employees have become very cynical about the prospects
of change. Recent efforts by executives to improve relationships
with employees have met with resistance and misunderstanding.
It has proven much more difficult to recapture the trust, or "social capital," once it was lost, than it was to develop in the first
place.

Whether change is planned or not, I argue that the single
most important problem for leaders of change is to maintain or
develop social capital, or motivational faith. Social capital may
be spent to buy patience and room to maneuver as those in the
organization try to adjust to environmental shifts and shocks.
However, leaders must realize that it can be used up.

At Precision Instruments, executives were apparently unaware that their social capital account was overdrawn. They
failed to recognize the importance of what they had, and they
were too busy to take note of changes in attitudes and feelings.

The following explication of some key components of motivational faith and the clues indicating its existence or dissipation should help others to avoid similar problems.

The Elements of Motivational Faith

Figure 2 shows the elements of motivational faith in an organization. Motivation to stay with an organization and give one's best to make the organization successful is based on beliefs about the future, on faith. Employees use their understanding of history, the promises made to them, and their own predisposition to trust others to decide how much effort they will give to the organization. If they have faith in the fairness and in the ability of the organization and in their own ability to make valued contributions, then they are very likely to be motivated to work for the good of the organization. They assume that their own excellent contributions to the organization will be noticed and rewarded appropriately. They therefore spend little time worrying about how to protect themselves and work hard to cooperate with others to make the organization succeed (see Ouchi, 1980, 1981; Wilkins and Ouchi, 1983).

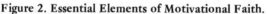

Figure 2. Essential Elements of Motivational Faith.

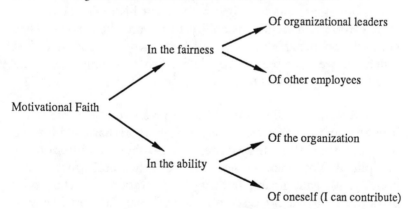

Figure 2 suggests four elements of motivational faith that help create organizational character. Such faith includes answers to questions about the fairness of organizational leaders and other employees and about the ability of the organization and of the individual. Let us consider briefly each of these elements.

Faith in the Fairness of Leaders. Most of us believe we have a right to expect that our leaders—whether in business, government, or other types of organizations—will use their power in the best interest of the organization. If they seek personal ends instead, then we believe that they have violated our trust. Indeed, as a people, we drove Richard Nixon from the U.S. presidency when we felt he acted illegally and self-servingly (Neustadt, 1980; Dalton and Thompson, 1986).

Of course, we do not, or cannot, always remove leaders from office when they betray our trust in them. However, to the extent that we lose confidence in them, they lose their power to influence us. Usually this loss of leadership power is subtle and appears only informally in leaders' increased need to use formal rewards and sanctions to get people to do what they want.

At Precision Instruments, we can see the erosion of social capital, or faith in the leaders, when leaders became unpredictable and seemed to turn a deaf ear to employee efforts to point to problems. Employees had previously trusted the president, Jim Hart, to personally approve all salary, promotion, and bonus decisions, but they began to doubt his understanding of their efforts and hence his ability to reward them fairly. They became convinced that Hart played favorites and had lost touch. As we have seen, many decided that the only way to ensure fair treatment was to bring in a union.

Faith in the Fairness of Employees. We also come to believe that an organization is not fair if we work hard and honestly while others shirk their duties or are dishonest without being disciplined. Yet when we see others call their colleagues on dishonesty, we gain greater faith in the operation of certain rules of fairness. Or when we see others work hard and creatively to keep important company commitments and protect the best interests of the organization, we are likely to be motivated to follow suit.

At Precision Instruments, employees began to see their co-workers cheat on their reports of rework and scrap rates. Many wondered what had happened to the old spirit of "all for one and one for all." Such examples of erosion of that spirit seriously depressed the faith of others.

Faith in the Ability of the Organization. When people come to believe that the company cannot deliver on its leaders' promises, the beliefs become self-fulfilling prophecies. People are not motivated to do what they can to make promises come true, and therefore they do not.

At Precision Instruments, faith in the organization eroded when management continued to press for shorter delivery times. Unwise promises were made for deliveries while poorer quality raw materials and unfamiliar new products significantly increased rework and production times. At first, employees complained that managers were unfair, but as they tried hard to rectify problems and develop their skills with little improvement, they began to lose pride and faith in the organization's ability. They stopped trying as hard as they had previously.

Faith in One's Own Ability. People who believe that their jobs will make a difference and that they can do what they are asked to do are likely to be more motivated than those who lack such beliefs. In addition, when people feel that they have the opportunity to grow, to make mistakes and learn from them, so they can eventually make valued contributions, they are more likely to continue to be motivated even when they fail occasionally. Of course, we are more motivated by these beliefs in our ability to contribute when we think they will be fairly noticed and rewarded. Faith in fairness is important, but without a confidence in our own ability, we are unlikely to try very hard.

Employees at Precision Instruments discovered that their sacrifices for the company were not particularly appreciated or effective. Their motivation to be creative and to develop new skills eroded along with this dissipation of faith in their ability to influence business results.

Uncovering Motivational Faith

Employees and managers are not always articulate about or completely conscious of the motivations and faith just discussed. Sometimes they are quite aware of these concerns, but are reticent to discuss them openly. As a result, it can be difficult to get completely accurate responses about faith in the organization. In the assessment resource at the end of this book, I discuss more specifically the difficulties of uncovering faith and the other components of organizational character. I also offer suggestions about concrete ways to overcome those difficulties. Here I suggest considering questions that overtly address the issues I have just presented. My intent is to illustrate concretely how each element may manifest itself. In many organizations where people are open and are encouraged to give feedback, these straightforward questions will be sufficient to generate insightful discussions about faith in the organization. They will help you determine the current level of social capital.

Questions About Motivational Faith

Faith in Leader Fairness

1. Are leaders perceived as working for the good of the whole or for their own selfish interests?
2. Do leaders seem to understand and represent the best interests of employees?
3. Do people believe leaders have a memory? That is, do they believe that when they make short-term sacrifices for the company their leaders will remember and recognize these sacrifices?
4. Do leaders recognize the difference between good and bad performance?
5. Do they take appropriate action to reward or punish fairly?
6. Do employees believe that leaders can work out differences of opinion between groups and individuals in appropriate ways?

Faith in the Fairness of Others

1. Do other employees take advantage of the company's trust and flaunt it?

2. Do other employees take it upon themselves to call others on their shirking or other dishonest behavior?
3. Do other employees seem to take seriously their responsibility to the company? Do they work hard and creatively to keep company commitments and protect the company's image?

Faith in Organizational Ability

1. Do people see the organization as being distinctively capable relative to competitors? Are they aware and proud of specific differences in capability?
2. Do people trust in the repair strategies that leaders use when problems occur?
3. Do people believe that leaders take seriously the input of members who describe problems from their local point of view?

Faith in Personal Ability

1. Do people feel that their job is important to the company's success?
2. Do employees feel that they are able to do what they are asked to do?
3. Do people feel that they can excel at their jobs?
4. When people make mistakes, do they feel that they can overcome and learn from them?
5. Do people see themselves as growing and improving through inevitable mistakes? Or do they fear that only one or two errors will get them "canned"?

Whether people in the organization decide to cooperate and work for the organization or protect themselves and their own self-interests depends on their answers to the preceding questions. Employees are often willing to give the organization a chance to see if it will be fair and competent and whether they will be recognized. But if, after some effort, they begin to believe that they need to protect themselves, then much of the energy, creativity, and flexibility the organization could enjoy is used up in self-protection.

The before and after comparison at Precision Instruments

suggests how much is lost when these questions are answered negatively for the organization. When trust is not an integral part of the relationship between organizational representatives and employees, both groups spend significant energy checking up on one another. Agreements must be written down and people held accountable to unvarying rules and procedures that do not fit unforeseen circumstances.

Many managers, executives, and employee groups engage in this kind of exchange. It seems to me that such organizations develop much more skill at producing cynicism than products or services. More effort and creativity go into claim and counterclaim and into snooping and spreading rumors than into building the organization.

Of course, some of the concerns about motivation and social capital are related to questions employees have about "who we are" as an organization. That is, employees may be motivated or even inspired by an understanding of how their organization is unique and how it embodies values they cherish. We now consider these aspects of a corporate character that have to do with shared vision.

Shared Vision

As I will describe in greater detail in Chapter Four, a common definition of company purpose and values can perform useful functions: (1) *inspiration* as people feel uplifted by the purpose, (2) *integration* because various groups see what they have in common and why they need to cooperate, and (3) *focus* that keeps the organization from drifting into wasteful activities.

Some people argue that it is hard to get really worked up over potato chips or petrochemicals. However, I have seen enough groups of people become involved in understanding customer needs and in taking pride in their work, whatever it was, that I doubt we can continue to make excuses for lack of enthusiasm and vision. Besides, many values beyond pride of products can serve to inspire and unite people. Indeed, in Chapter Four we will examine values that appear to motivate broad groups of people, no matter what the product or service, such as doing excellent work or being of service.

The most important lesson for managers is the recent research finding that the most successful firms tend more often to mention values in addition to making a profit as their purpose. Profit is important, but it is insufficient to unite, guide, and inspire large groups of people by itself. In addition, there are many ways to make a profit, only some of which are within the capacity and interest of a given organization. Hence, defining competitive domains and ethical constraints can help managers and employees prioritize and focus their efforts (Ouchi, 1981; Pearce and David, 1987).

Potential Content of a Shared Vision

A shared vision can address at least four areas: (1) a general concept of the business, (2) a sense of uniqueness or identity, (3) a philosophy about employee relationships, (4) an orientation to external stakeholders (shareholders, regulatory agencies, and the general public). I will consider briefly each of these areas in turn and then suggest questions for managers to ask to determine the existence and nature of related employee beliefs.

Note that I am *not* suggesting what should be included in a written or public statement of mission. For reasons of complexity, of potential misunderstanding, or of concerns about how much information to let the public and competitors know, many of the items described below probably should not be written in a formal statement. Instead, I focus on the operating vision of a group of people. That is, our concern is to determine the kinds of perspectives and beliefs that currently direct choices and actions in the organization. We want to know the extent to which beliefs are shared and how they relate to changes the organization needs to make. (Chapter Four looks specifically at the functions and dysfunctions of written statements of philosophy or vision. Such a statement may be a useful tool to influence existing operating beliefs, but is useless and even detrimental in the absence of such beliefs.)

A Concept of the Business. A vision that gives broad direction to decisions in an organization might include some beliefs about the keys to success or to avoiding pitfalls. Such ideas might indicate the kind of business the company wants to be in, the ways it adds value to customers, the critical challenges it faces from competitors, the key strengths (technologies, skills) of the organization, and how the firm meets its challenges and opportunities.

Employees at Precision Instruments, even in manufacturing and clerical positions, shared some general understandings about what their firm did well and therefore what their priorities should be. They understood that much of the firm's success derived from an innovative design for their measurement instruments, which allowed many different instruments to be assembled from the same basic and interchangeable parts. As a result, customers did not have to store large inventories of specialized parts, and the company could produce high-quality parts very efficiently. Employees understood the importance of delivering high-quality, low-cost parts quickly to customers who kept their inventories low and ordered when they needed something.

The problems started when new, more specialized products were developed that did not fit the old concept. Management still believed that it could promise quick delivery and high quality. However, the firm began to use some different suppliers whose material was less reliable. It also had employees working on new and more specialized products that required shorter production cycles and more set-up time. Employees did not understand why the company was producing these new products in the first place. In addition, they felt the old values of quality and meeting delivery promises were being violated consistently. They came to view management requests for improvement cynically.

A Sense of Identity. What makes one organization different from others? We come to know who we are as much by understanding who we are not—how we differ from others—as by anything else. Is a company the best in quality, in developing new products, in providing service? Is it unique in the way it develops employees? Employees often make such comparisons as ways of understanding who they are.

Employees at Precision Instruments had taken great pride in the quality of their work and in meeting tight delivery commitments, but they became frustrated and then cynical about these very areas. They came to believe that they were not much different from other firms except that some other firms had the help of a union to keep management honest.

A Philosophy of Employee Relationships. As a matter of shared vision and motivational faith, employees must connect broad purpose and how to accomplish it. Otherwise, the company's success and its fairness with employees become disconnected. We want to know, then, how connected such ideas are. We are interested in whether people in the organization see the long-term development of employees as important. We want to know whether employees see one another as competitors, team members, partners, or members of different classes.

Before the move, Precision Instruments' employees felt that they were part of a family. People referred to the company as "us" and "we" and "our." They believed that management was interested in their insights and that they had the opportunity to improve their skills and progress in the company. They also felt that their contribution was strategically important. However, when Phelps left and the company started to focus on new products and moved into a new building, they detected real changes. The building reflected clear class differences, and new managers and new design engineers were brought in from the outside. They treated older employees coldly. For example, Phelps's replacement spent little time in the manufacturing area and sent memos to inform people of changes he decided on rather than talking things through with people.

All of these changes led employees to alter their beliefs about their role in the company. They referred to the company and management as "them" and came to assume that management was not particularly interested in listening to them or helping them to develop in the company. Paradoxically, they also assumed that their contributions were no longer considered critical to strategy at a time when management felt employee reticence was the major constraint on profits.

Orientation to External Stakeholders. Beyond the orientation to employees, managers need to discover what people believe about their relationships to customers, suppliers, shareholders, regulatory agencies, the communities in which they live, and other relevant groups. In some organizations, a clear sense of the group's role in society provides considerable direction to the choices people make and the priorities they set.

The primary external stakeholders that employees at Precision Instruments spoke about were customers and suppliers. Originally, they felt they understood the company's relationship to both groups. They became disillusioned, however, when managers seemed unwilling to pass on their feedback about supply quality to suppliers and when management made unrealistic promises to customers that they were sure the company could not meet. As a result, they were increasingly unsure about the role they should play with external groups.

Uncovering Shared Vision

Perhaps the most important thing to be learned from watching operating beliefs about vision change at Precision Instruments is that changes occurred because of changed practices, not changed rhetoric. Managers continued to espouse the same values and principles as before, but daily practices gave their statements the lie. In particular, the role of liaison and interpreter between management and manufacturing that Phelps had played was not replaced when he left. He had spent time helping employees understand the changes in the firm's challenges so that they understood the reasons behind changes in practice. He helped crystalize the firm's identity by showing employees how unique the company was and what was at stake in keeping its commitments. Employees came to feel that the firm's commitments were their commitments. They saw the link between grand ideas and daily practices (Davis, 1984).

Sometimes beliefs about the role, mission, and operation of the company are implicit. That is, people take them for granted and do not talk about them much. As a result, I find that asking managers and others to answer direct questions about beliefs is not as helpful as having them talk about what they do and what they have done. For example, I ask managers to talk about the history of the organization starting back as far as they can recall. I ask them to talk about the founding, significant changes, choice of successor(s), products, strategies, financing, successes, and failures—whatever they think is relevant to understanding how the business works. I also ask them to talk about what has changed in their business environment and what current challenges and opportunities they think result from those changes.

While they talk about current and past practice in several areas, I listen for implications relevant to the areas we have just considered. I have the following questions in mind and occasionally ask one or several of them if the topic comes up. Once managers start thinking about concrete past and current events, they find it much easier to consider these questions.

Questions About Shared Vision

Concept of the Business

1. What business are we in? Are there limitations to the kinds of businesses we can or want to be in?
2. What do we have to do well to compete or succeed?
3. How do we add value to customers? How does that differ from what competitors do?
4. What are our most critical challenges?
5. What are our most important opportunities?

Corporate Identity

1. Who are our major competitors?
2. In what ways are we unique? Which of these areas of uniqueness are we proud about? Which are we embarrassed or worried about?
3. What are our relative strengths and weaknesses?

Philosophy of Managing People

1. What do employees want or deserve in exchange for their efforts—security, promotion, share of profits, high wages, ownership?
2. How important are employees to our success? Are some categories of employees more important than others?
3. How do employees see one another—as partners, competitors, friends?
4. What do we believe about the importance of developing skills as opposed to hiring skills?

Orientation to Stakeholders

1. Who are the most important stakeholders?
2. What is our relationship to each of these groups? Do we learn from them, compete with them, or try to fool them?
3. What do we believe about their view of us? Are we trustworthy, dishonest, or hard bargainers?

Of course, if the organization does not develop and update its skill, then faith in the organization and shared vision are in vain. We must also assess the current skill of the organization.

Distinctive Skills

Distinctive skills are the most ignored aspect of character and the most difficult component of character to describe. A well-developed skill consists of much more than organizational structure and systems or employees' individual skills. Indeed, much of an organization's skill resides in the intangible motivation of employees to make something work no matter what. I have suggested that the motivational component of competence is most directly related to faith in fairness and ability. However, equally important and intangible are the largely tacit and often unspoken understandings and habits of various people throughout an organization.

A manager needs to understand at least three ideas about organizational skills to see how to support, change, and develop them: (1) skills reside in the experience and tacit intuitions, memories, and routines of groups of people that are learned and remembered by doing, (2) skills are found in complex and varied groupings of individuals and depend on the quality of their connections and relationships, and (3) know-how may or may not be perpetuated depending on the selection, training, reward, and retention processes of the organization.

After elaborating on each of these ideas, I will suggest the kinds of questions executives might pose to apply these insights to their own assessment of corporate character.

Distinctive Skills Are Tacit. Having an organizational skill is something like being able to type: most of the skill is in the fingers, is remembered by doing, and is done more efficiently if one does not think about everything but just does it. That is, when organizations develop a unique competence, the relevant people will know how to perform the complex behaviors involved but they often will be unable to tell you everything that is required to perform the skill, because it will have become second nature (Polanyi, 1958; Nelson and Winters, 1982).

Consider this example of the tacitness of organizational skill. For over twenty years, Hewlett-Packard (HP) honed its employees' skills related to developing high-quality computer hardware for sophisticated engineering or scientific communities. During the past five or six years, HP executives have been struggling to develop additional skills required by the new markets they have entered. Among other things, these new markets require that HP develop software to integrate system components and make them compatible.

A few years ago, an HP manager tried to describe to me the difference between being competent and struggling to become competent. He chose to contrast the firm's skills at hardware development with its skills in developing software: "Let's imagine that you went to one of our division general managers and asked him about the possibility of delivering a particular piece of hardware that was similar to but not exactly like anything HP has done. Within a few hours, and in some cases within only a few minutes, this manager would be able to tell you the cost of the equipment, how long it would take to work out the bugs and have a working model, and whether it made any sense for HP to try to make it for you. The reason it might take a little longer sometimes is that this general manager, typically an electrical engineer with long experience at the company, might not have all the details at his fingertips. But in that case, he would know who did know and could consult them quickly."

Contrast this situation with the condition at that time regarding software development skills, according to my contact. If you were to ask a division general manager about developing some software to improve system compatibility, you would probably get some stalling and a lot of guesswork. The manager would be unsure of the level of difficulty and consequent costs and timing involved. The manager would also take more time to find out who could really help answer these questions and would not be as clear about whether this kind of project would make sense for HP.

This contrast of competencies at HP demonstrates that skill takes time to develop and consists of the residue of experiences. The skill will indeed be readily available in the fingers and memories of lots of individuals, but no one person is likely to know all the details. Rather, they will have a sense of who knows what and generally how to work with these people to obtain all the details. Some individuals will be more crucial than others.

The tacitness of organizational skills has several implications. First, the more tacit and intuitive the skill, the more difficult it will be to pass on. This is both good news and bad news. It is good news because competitors will have a similarly difficult task, and if you have already developed some level of skill and continue to perpetuate it, then the skill can be a significant competitive advantage (Barney, 1986; Lippman and Rumelt, 1982). However, the bad news is that new employees will require time to acquire skills that are hard to communicate concretely (Wilkins and Ouchi, 1983). They will need on-the-job experience and will need to build relationships and earn trust before they can be said to have this kind of organizational skill. Managers must, therefore, be certain that the skills they choose to perpetuate add value to the firm. They would also be wise to have at least some representatives in top management who have an intuitive feel for the firm's most critical skills.

Know-How Networks. Competence in an organization can rarely be traced to a single individual. Organizational competence typically resides in the relationships, norms, memories, habits, and collective skills of a network of people. However, for a particular problem, the composition of the network may differ significantly. For example, those who can really contribute to customizing a product will differ depending on the product and the particular customer needs. And customizing skills may form around a collection of people from R&D, marketing, production, purchasing, and general management, while achieving quality may additionally include manufacturing, top management, and design engineering.

The problem is that organizations may often inhibit rather than facilitate the largely informal and flexible networking needed to get such diverse groups of people to cooperate comfortably. In the name of control and efficiency, managers create structures, reward systems, and physical settings that separate people into functional or product groupings. Such groupings can inhibit the right people from knowing or having access to others and keep them from feeling comfortable about working with people from diverse locations.

For example, at Precision Instruments, management did not appreciate how much of a role Harold Phelps played in being aware of the tacit aspects of production and knowing who needed to be involved in what kinds of problems. Without his influence, production capabilities and insights were not brought to bear on problems to the same extent. Commitments for delivery on products were made unwisely and on products that had not been fully developed with collaboration between production and design engineering. Beyond that, the layout of the new building separated people who needed to work together and created a two-class system that inhibited communication.

The implication for managers is that if they want to protect, develop, or change organizational skills, then they must become aware of the more tacit aspects of their competence. They must become more aware of who knows what and how to get the right people together to solve different problems. Developing appropriate relationships (trust) and overcoming the inhibitions of structures, rewards, and physical settings are critical to maintaining and developing organizational competence.

In this same vein, executives should know whether there are contacts outside the firm that contribute to its competence. For example, John Kotter (1982) found that effective general managers had literally thousands of contacts within an industry that helped them to make sense of trends and see possibilities. The skill of these managers resided in part in their contacts, and they were not as skillful when they were transplanted into other industries.

Distinctive Skills Can Be Hard to Perpetuate. The kind of organizational know-how I am talking about can be the key to organizational competitiveness both because people get really good at something and because it is so difficult for other firms to imitate. However, because the know-how consists of tacit understandings and habits based on extensive trial-and-error experience and on relationships among a number of people, it can be very difficult to pass on to others. Managers will also find it difficult to appropriately value and support such competencies because they are so tacit.

Of concern, then, is whether organizational skills will disintegrate over time. That is, are new people selected, developed, rewarded, and encouraged to take part in producing a particular know-how? And do managers help or hinder the perpetuation of particular competencies by what they value, how consistent their focus is, how they make transfers and promotions, and whom they consult with?

For example, the president of a large electronics firm explained to me how his company was developing the ability to transfer technology rapidly to high-quality manufactured products. He announced this area as one of high priority, selected only the finest people from several other areas to work on the problem, and paid significant attention to their efforts. Now everyone seems to want to be involved in what was previously seen as a low-priority problem.

What is clear to the president is that the company is making significant improvement toward new skills in technology transfer. What may be less clear is that a focus on one area may mean less focus somewhere else. What skills are eroded in the process? And what kinds of incompetencies result from a particular focus? That is, a focus on R&D may lead the firm to pay less attention to cost-cutting efficiencies because it relies on flexibility and invention rather than on efficiency to compete.

Beyond the protection, attention, or neglect of top management, other factors may allow for or discourage the development and perpetuation of a particular competence. For example, patents, unique relationships with universities, or monopoly conditions due to market-share position or government protection should be considered.

Uncovering Organizational Skills

Any valuable organizational skill becomes elaborated over time and includes not only specific rules, organizational systems, or clear procedures but also more complex perspectives, intuitions, and abilities that are based on varied experience in applying the knowledge in many situations. To understand and change organizational skills, we must look to the memories, habits, routines, intuitions, and networks of experienced people.

Frankly, organizational know-how of the sort I have been discussing is very difficult to capture. I have tried for some time to develop questions that would help managers see the components of such competence. However, I have discovered that because the key aspects of competence are often based on tacit intuitions, habits, and relationships, managers who would understand it must be somewhat intuitive as well.

This problem is akin to that of the basketball coach who would like to understand and perpetuate the skill of his championship team. Of course, he can focus on the particular individuals on the team, but some teams have highly skilled individuals who never learn to work together. Or he could pay close attention to the formal plays they use or the strategies he uses for substitution. However, teams have to adapt plays to fit what the other team allows and to take advantage of fleeting moments of inattention or weakness by the defense. Unless the coach develops a strong feel for how different combinations of players work to produce particular outcomes, the relationships between players, and the unique strengths they develop as a group because of shared experiences, he will miss the most important aspects of the team's competence. His best chance to comprehend the competence is to spend a lot of time with the team and work on these intangibles as well as the more formal aspects of the team's competence.

I believe that the best way for managers to understand their organization's competencies is for them to spend time with those who do the work and be observant and interested. Of course, some management teams are composed of people who have had different backgrounds in the firm. Sometimes their past experience in the firm with particular groups provides them with an intuitive feel for the operations within the firm. Their greatest need, then, is to periodically update their feel for the business. However, all members of the team need to find ways to be in touch with the nuts and bolts of organizational skill.

The questions I suggest below can be asked directly, but are best answered through thoughtful observation by managers who spend time occasionally in the field. In the resource, I suggest ways that several managers of my acquaintance have found to get in touch with the more tacit aspects of organizational skills.

Questions About Distinctive Skills

Tacit Aspects of Skills

1. What do we do very well? What do we seem to be able to do with our eyes closed? What do we have some good intuition about?
2. What kinds of capabilities do we have the hardest time passing on to our new employees?
3. What do we do poorly? Where does our intuition seem to fail us?

Know-How Networks

1. Are local managers and other employees able to find the right people to involve in the problems they face?

2. Do those with questions on particular problems know whom to talk to and have easy access to these people?
3. What contacts external to the firm are important to our competence—suppliers, customers, experts? Do we have and use access to these people?

Skill Perpetuation

1. How are new people selected, developed, trained?
2. Are newcomers personally developing skills that contribute?
3. Are newcomers forming relationships with and awareness of important networks so that their skills add up to organizational know-how?
4. Do more mature members of the organization accept and help to develop newcomers?
5. To which competencies do executives seem to give most attention and resources?
6. Are some competencies eroding through lack of attention, involvement, and support of management?
7. What external contacts are critical to our know-how? Are we developing these contacts?

How Character Components Relate to Change

Most managers and executives who take time to assess their corporate character will be interested in the implications of their assessment for organizational improvement. I have set off this discussion of how character assessment relates to change to give it greater emphasis. However, the questions I suggest in the following discussion can be asked when the other questions about the current character are asked.

Motivational Faith and Change. As we saw with the example of Stop and Shop (Chapter One), when people have faith that they will be given an opportunity and support to make changes, they can change quickly. The critical concern for those contemplating change, then, is what people in their units expect to happen in times of change. Perhaps the best information people have for their expectations is history. That is, we can learn much about their expectations by asking them to tell us what they remember or what they have heard about past changes. In addition, we can ask people to predict what will happen in the event of major changes to understand their fears and hopes. Here I am interested in how people see the politics of the organization. Who sides with whom, and what are the implications for me and my group depending on who "wins"? Is the organization likely to lay people off? If it does, then what help will it give me to find a new job and what are my prospects? If I am not released, then will I have a chance to have an influence on future changes and time to adapt? Will we be able to change fast enough to make the organization successful? These are the kinds of questions I hear from people in organizations facing significant change. They often find answers in history and in the current actions of management.

Shared Vision and Change. As we saw in Chapter One, many organizational efforts to change fail because people do not share a sense of a need for change, cannot agree on what to try, or fail to give an alternative a fair chance. With these problems in mind, we should be concerned about two kinds of insights about the beliefs people hold regarding a company's purpose, role, and mission: (1) Do the current beliefs about the organization's challenges and opportunities fit with our sense of the realities the company (or unit) faces? and (2) What views are shared, if any, about the seriousness of our need to change and the kinds of solutions that are favored?

Managers might also ask some skill questions that apply to shared vision. How do people in this organization learn about the challenges, opportunities, and appropriate mission of the organization? What relationships or skill deficiencies inhibit learning in these areas? Organizations where people regularly update their maps of the organization's challenges and opportunities are more likely to have practiced discussing their beliefs and coming to general consensus about those beliefs. For example, at Motorola executives at the corporate level never develop a strategic plan per se. However, they regularly engage in "strategic renewal" every twelve to eighteen months. They review the environments in which they compete, consider alternative scenarios for what might happen in those environments, and consider their own company's strengths and weaknesses. They try to come up with a "strategic intent" that will guide "down-the-line" managers in developing more specific short-term plans.

Organizational Skills and Change. Executives should also be interested in how dynamic the various competencies in their firm are. That is, organizations vary in how innovative, active, and responsive people learn to be in adapting to and recovering from problems.

We considered in Chapter One how Stop and Shop developed competence, at least among general managers, to adapt management style in the face of new needs. Specifically, they have learned how to communicate openly about the problems they face, jointly determine appropriate responses, and engage in the development of new skills through training, developing new systems and structures, and rewarding improvements.

Because organizations may develop different processes for change, our chief concern should be to learn the organization's repair strategies and specific change skills. Using comfortable change processes at least to start change may be helpful. For example, at a state-of-the-art computer firm, executives have learned to rely on a few designated "idea" people. These employees have been successful in the past in figuring out where the industry was going and in convincing others about appropriate responses. This company is vulnerable to kinds of changes that their idea people do not understand, of course, but the company tends to respond quickly to changes the idea people do understand. However, anyone seeking to change this organization must know about the designated idea people and develop their support of the changes.

Other differences in how the firm or groups within it adapt may have to do with the way the group learns about problems. That is, do people have ways to measure the results of their efforts and do they look for new ways? Or do they tend to wait for a crisis to teach them what to attend to? How open are people to different perspectives?

Answers to these questions will be critical for those interested in change. For example, organizations that rely on financial or operational data to determine the need for adaptation can develop new measures to help people see new needs. However, sometimes the most important changes cannot be measured. For instance, in one company that relied on long-term contracts with military groups, the managers did not see financial results of their efforts for three or four years. They had to base their judgments about the current well-being or troubles of the organization on less tangible understandings of their business such as current legislation and attitudes of contracting officials.

Beyond differences in the process of adaptation, firms may also differ in the content of their competence in ways that affect how adaptive they are. For instance, the firm that encourages people to focus on rules and procedures as reasons for what they do rather than on principles, perspective, and understanding of the big picture (that is, on a shared and dynamic vision) is likely to discourage adaptation.

The resource at the end of this book suggests in much greater detail the problems of uncovering organizational character and how to address them. It also contains specific suggestions about how managers and others may use the questions about character presented in this chapter to start developing the character of an organization. Of course, each organization will be different in needs, skills, faith, and vision. The particular steps managers take in developing character will need to be customized. However, in Chapter Three, I suggest that all efforts to change should pay attention to how changes affect motivational faith. I also show the diversity of approaches managers in a variety of companies have used to start developing character.

3

Change the Organization
Without Losing Character

For many years, the business press has chronicled how AT&T's executives have tried to create a marketing orientation and marketing skills—efforts that have apparently met with resistance. Even before divestiture of local operating companies, CEO Charles Brown called for increased emphasis on meeting customer needs rather than the long-term preeminent concern for delivering efficient service. Most top managers seemed to agree with the need for change. New training programs were created, and the organization was restructured to focus more attention on market segments.

Initially, AT&T violated its traditional policy of promoting from within, bringing in new role models from other companies. For example, Arch McGill from IBM was hired as vice president of business marketing. Many saw McGill as the antithesis of a "Bell-shaped man" because of his adversarial style and his reputation as an innovator. He incessantly preached to marketers his new slogan, "I make the difference," encouraging them to be entrepreneurs. He reinforced the idea with incentives that pitted salespeople against each other to earn bonuses, a system previously unknown at AT&T.

But change was slow. Three years after McGill came to AT&T, the *Wall Street Journal* ("Bell Battles: AT&T Marketing . . . ," 1984) reported strong evidence that marketing executives and manufacturing veterans were locked in a power struggle for control of the company and that manufacturers had gained the upper hand. Manufacturers, not marketers, moved into the corporation's pivotal jobs under a top-level reorganization in December of 1983, consolidating their hold on strategy, introductions of new products, and day-to-day operations. Three of AT&T's senior marketing executives had left the company during the previous six months, along with several other marketing managers.

How could so much consensus about the need to create marketing skills result in so much effort and so little apparent change?

Those who have developed a distinctive corporate character frequently greet significant changes with significant resistance. Such resistance often stems less from a denial of the need to change than from uncertainty about specifically how to accomplish the change. As I argued in the first chapter, resistance can come when people feel cut off from the past and thus lose their sense of who they are, of how to behave, and of how they will be rewarded.

The Need to Change Versus a Crisis in Faith

One of the most difficult aspects of changing an organization and developing new character traits stems from a critical tension: The very situation that clearly reveals the need to change and produces enough motivation to change may create a crisis in the faith people have that they can make things work.

Because significant change in an organization is so difficult and people are so ready to resist change in what has become functional for them, there needs to be strong motivation to change. This motivation often comes from a crisis, a situation in which people sense that their cherished values or habits no longer work. AT&T has faced such crises. However, this sense of crisis and discounting of one's traditions are likely to lead to self-doubt.

What people believe about the future becomes a self-fulfilling prophecy. If they believe that the organization cannot be changed, that the organization cannot meet the challenges it faces, then they are right. They are right, in part, because their expectations about the future lead to lower motivation and thus reduced effort. When people see themselves confronting novel problems for which they will have no ready answers, they tend to resist change all the more.

Managers who would change their organizations must therefore deal with an uneasy tension: How can they develop enough concern about the current situation while still encouraging a feeling that the world is not a completely blank slate? They can manage this tension if they help people use appropriate skills, insights, and values of the past to move forward.

From this point of view, AT&T executives may have finally discovered what they should have been doing all along. Bringing in outsiders to develop a marketing orientation is fraught with the risks considered in Chapter One. A better strategy may be to require that the manufacturing and operating people acquire new marketing skills while still paying attention to how their past traditions and skills apply. Of course, honoring the past in this way risks not changing enough, but bringing in outside marketing people did not accomplish the desired change in character either.

In this chapter I will consider how several companies have attempted significant changes without repudiating the past or acting entirely out of character. Their assumption, in most cases, was that more change can be accomplished with much less resistance if executives do not directly attack the current corporate character.

The question, then, becomes: "How can we take advantage of our past learning, values, and traditions to develop answers to future problems?" The current organizational character often provides the answer. It consists of what motivates people and consequently suggests what themes and strategies can energize large groups of people. It also consists of certain skills that can be applied to many different problems.

The previous chapter described how organizational character can suggest answers to questions about the level of social capital and therefore the trust people put in their leaders. Understanding the current vision of managers and others helps determine how ready people are for change. Understanding organizational skills can suggest the kinds of change processes people understand best and those that they have tried and discarded. Answers to these questions should provide us with a number of suggestions about where to start and whom to start with in making needed changes.

Because each company is different, we must take into account the specific nuances, competencies, and differences residing in each organization. Hence, those who seek significant change in organizational character need not a set of suggestions that can be universally applied but rather a list of things others have tried, from which they can choose what will fit their own organization.

I offer two lists of ways to get started with significant changes. One is concerned with the past and the other with the future, but both demonstrate sensitivity to the constraints and opportunities suggested by an organization's character.

Honoring the Past	*Growing in New Ways*
Return to the past for inspiration and instruction.	Allow things to grow in new ways.
Repent and reform.	Reward efforts in the right direction.
Identify the principles that will remain constant.	Create punctuated evolution and reserves.
Find current examples of success within the company.	Experiment.
Promote hybrids.	Consider therapy.
Label eras.	Use "selective surgery."
Mourn the loss of a cherished past.	

The list on the left provides several examples of how various organizations have managed to honor their past—how they have reassured those devoted to traditions and energized those hoping for change without destroying a sense of pride and appreciation for what has been accomplished. The list on the right indicates how companies have started growing in new ways without unduly challenging the past. A company considering significant change would be well advised to learn from both lists: to both honor the past and learn how to grow in new ways.

Of course, none of the actions I have listed was sufficient to produce all the change a company sought. Some of the companies started to change well but have not continued well. The continuation of significant efforts to change and the establishment of new direction for the corporate character are subjects for a subsequent section. I focus here only on the problem of how to get started without creating large-scale resistance or loss of faith in the ability of the company and its employees. Indeed, the examples cited below are best thought of as ways companies have helped people start to think about change—about why it is necessary and how it will be approached generally.

How to Honor the Past

1. *Return to the past for inspiration and instruction:* Simplot, a major producer of french fries for McDonald's, has in recent years encouraged a "return to the example of our founder, Jack Simplot, who was a true entrepreneur." Their business originally skyrocketed when they became associated with the growth of McDonald's. Accompanying this growth was a feeling of security and a lack of innovation that the company would like to overcome now that the growth of McDonald's has leveled off. The strategy is to hold up Jack Simplot's entrepreneurial example for emulation by other employees.

Tektronix has used a similar tactic. Kim Fisher (1986), an internal management and organization development consultant at Tektronix, has written recently about how the late Howard Vollum, one of the founders of Tektronix, tried to implement participative management in parts of the company. Participative management is not new, Vollum said in effect: "It was here at the start. Then we kind of got away from it. I think it's very important that we get back to it." Fisher writes that "these . . . visible statements by respected leaders can make the journey more like coming home than jumping off a cliff into the unknown" (1986, p. 466).

Some years ago, Imperial Oil was confronted with a serious

need to reduce its payroll. Company executives originally intended to lay off a large number of employees. However, human resource professionals suggested that the company examine its history to discover how it had dealt with business cycle swings previously. The company had a history of long-term employment and a significant feeling of family. Upon investigating its history, the executives discovered that the company had often offered early retirement and worked at relocating employees rather than laying people off. They decided to remind employees of the company's tradition to indicate a desire to continue the same feeling of loyalty to the company, and then suggest traditions of the past and additional similar practices that would allow them to avoid layoffs and still reduce their payroll.

The response to these efforts was tremendous, in terms of both the number of people who wanted to take advantage of the opportunities offered and an increase in the loyalty and sense of pride in the company among employees. In this case, a tradition that had been attenuated over the years was reinforced and used to solve current problems.

2. *Repent and reform:* Rather than the positive cast given to the preceding efforts, some companies or managers have decided to admit that they have strayed from a correct path. Honoring the past, in this sense, does not entail maintaining the past practices but taking responsibility for, and admitting the existence of, past problems. It means renegotiating relationships and expectations so that organization members see the possibility of moving beyond the past.

I admire the courage of the manager of a huge manufacturing plant in a machine tools company. Competition from the Japanese and a strong dollar, which hurt exports, led many in his company to realize how much the often hostile relations with labor constrained their ability to improve productivity. Although he had been plant manager for only a year, he realized he was part of a system of management that was to some extent responsible for the hostile relations. He and his management team interviewed their subordinates in management and spent time with employees trying to assess the character of their organization.

The management team became aware how their own decisions passed on the intimidation they felt from the corporation. They also began to understand why they continued to hear stories about abusive plant executives who had not been around for eight years. While the current plant managers did not yell at people and threaten them, they usually focused on what was wrong with various departments and rarely noticed improvements. They were seen as a continuation of the previous management style because they were just more sophisticated in pressuring people. In addition, employees had not forgiven past abuses because no one had repented of them.

Realizing this state of affairs, the plant manager began a series of "renegotiating the relationship" meetings. He recognized his role in passing on pressure and expressed his willingness to change. The effect has been refreshing. Many employees have taken an attitude of wait and see, but the new openness about past problems and willingness to work through them has encouraged many employees and supervisors to recognize their own roles in the past hostilities and to begin to rethink their relationship.

In the unionized plant of a consumer goods company, managers concluded that major changes were essential to make the plant profitable. However, the union representatives were unwilling to make concessions. Managers learned that the union people did not believe management's arguments about problems. They pointed to several past events where they felt they had been told untruths. Managers sat down with these representatives and asked what would convince them. The union representatives asked to see the books of the plant. This request was unheard of. Obviously, the union could use the books in future bargaining. Managers decided that to receive trust they would have to give trust. They opened the books. They also invited the vice president in charge of new products to come and share his concerns about using the plant to produce new products because of its high costs of operation. The situation did not change overnight, but this was the beginning of a very different relationship. Faith in fairness grew steadily, and the new relationship allowed significant changes in work rules, which eventually resulted in improved plant performance.

Other companies have used a back-to-basics theme in their efforts to change a straying organization. This approach works best following repentance or when a new manager is appointed who was not responsible for the straying. One human resource professional told me of his experience at General Electric (GE) when a new manager was brought into a division that had become passive. The new manager, who had a significant history at GE, was quick to implement many of the budgeting and reporting practices that were common to the rest of the company. In addition, he instituted daily reporting meetings wherein each of the people directly reporting to him had to say what he or she had accomplished that day and how he or she had helped to reduce the production backlog and quality problems the division was facing. These and other activities helped him make clear that the division was moving back to basics.

Within months, the division had begun to change significantly. Part of the reason for the relative speed of this change was that the change involved reinstating a way of operating that had previously existed within that division. Even more helpful was the fact that this way of operating was an ongoing reality in the rest of the company.

3. *Identify the principles that will remain constant:* Hewlett-Packard (HP) demonstrates yet another way to maintain character in the face of change. HP executives recognize the company's need to learn to market to customers who differ from the sophisticated engineer who has been their bread and butter in the past. They also know that they need to coordinate better their development of large systems and of integrated pricing strategies. But such improvement requires changes in corporate character. And HP executives have been working on these problems for years. While not all employees have been pleased with the company's efforts to change, recent surveys at HP suggest a continuing level of loyalty and the expectation that the company will continue to be an excellent employer.

The company has accomplished this continued loyalty by making every effort to continue the "HP way" (their overt statement of character), even though it includes an emphasis on decentralized operation and autonomous management of divisions. As the development of large systems has required increased coordination between divisions, the company has tried to increase the number of meetings and coordinating efforts of division general managers, while still allowing some autonomy and encouraging the same concern for employee welfare. By focusing on what will remain unchanged, and showing that these commitments will be kept inviolate, the company has apparently been able to significantly improve coordination between divisions.

Centralized operation is obviously the textbook solution to the coordination problems at HP. Indeed, if HP continues to grow in the computer and systems area, it will have to develop much better skills in coordination. The current efforts are only a beginning. However, they represent a beginning that considers organizational character and employee loyalties.

4. *Find current examples of success within the company:* Much of the popularity of *In Search of Excellence,* by Thomas Peters and Robert Waterman (1982), stems from its use of yet another means of encouraging significant change. When experts on Japan say that American companies are inferior, U.S. managers often respond by saying, "Japanese management style might work for Japan, but we can't do it here." In contrast, Peters and Waterman held up excellent American companies for emulation. The result was an increase of pride in U.S. businesses and a motivation to improve. Within companies the same strategy has been effective.

In a recent study of a financial institution, I characterized the dominant management style in one company as "productivity through pressure." However, I discovered some highly regarded managers who achieved productivity that at least equaled the productivity of others, involved their employees in meeting company goals, and obtained high motivation and morale. These exceptional managers exemplified a style that accommodated hard-nosed concerns for output and also encouraged the involvement and growth of subordinates.

By chance, management received the results of an employee attitude survey at about the same time. The report presented a very negative picture of many employees feeling alienated and ready to leave the company. My findings suggested that these feelings were real but that there were alternatives already "in character" that could serve as models for change. The employee attitude survey results were met with great defensiveness and frustration. However, my findings were met with a strong desire to change, perhaps in large measure because the changes implied did not seem overwhelming.

5. *Promote hybrids:* The previous principle could be extended by promoting individuals who could serve as positive examples and putting them in charge. Edgar Schein (1985) calls this change process "hybridization." He suggests that, in many instances, companies may promote from within their ranks people who are currently accepted to some extent but who also differ from others in significant ways. General Electric provides an excellent recent example of this strategy.

Several years ago, John F. Welch was appointed CEO of GE. He arrived at this position when GE was accused of becoming overly cautious, and he championed the idea that people should take greater risks and not be managed by their budgets. In comparison to his predecessor, Reginald Jones, Welch is considered outgoing and gregarious. Jones was considered a more reserved and cautious risk taker who scrutinized every detail. Welch is viewed as being much more adventuresome and much more of a gambler. Welch has gone about the company selling the idea that the old management system was strong and rigid enough to prevent major mistakes, but he has emphasized that it has also stifled enterprise and cooled innovation ("General Electric—Going with the Winners," 1984).

Thus, Welch illustrates the idea of hybridization. He is viewed not as someone who would completely dismantle GE's corporate character but as someone who, while aware of past commitments, political interests, and organizational skills, would be willing and apparently able to move GE in a different direction.

6. *Label eras:* Another way of relating to the past, and yet moving and changing, is to picture the organization's history as being divided into eras (Peters, 1978). When a change is necessary, the management group and others seek to understand

and name a past era and then label the upcoming era. The result is that employees gain a sense that changes are needed without denigrating past efforts. Past efforts may have been appropriate to a previous era, with its particular needs, but a new era may require new approaches.

For example, the past administrator of a hospital system had engaged in significant building projects and was regarded by employees as a "brick and mortar man" rather than a health care professional. When the new administrator was brought in, he quickly sized up the situation and labeled the past era as a "building and development" phase. He suggested that the new phase would focus on consolidation and elaboration of the professional skills of the hospital system. Most of the people in the system accepted this labeling of eras.

In the nine years that followed, the new administrator presided over the construction of as much square footage as had the previous administrator in his twenty years. What started out with great enthusiasm and willingness from employees resulted in significant employee distrust of administrators. The critical constraint to significant change was not the new administrator. He was sincere and made great efforts to attend to health care professionalism. The problem was that he had kept the management team that the previous administrator had chosen. This group gave lip service to professional growth, but what it knew and implemented was building hospital facilities. This example suggests both the usefulness of starting with the right image of what is to be done and the difficulty of implementing the envisioned change.

7. *Mourn the loss of a cherished past:* Terrence Deal (1985) has offered numerous examples that illustrate how hard it is for people to give up what they have learned to cherish. Before we leave this section on ways of honoring the past, it is appropriate to acknowledge the need people have to mourn what must be left behind.

Studies of death and dying suggest that in these experiences of loss people have two somewhat conflicting needs. The first is the need to mourn for what has been lost. The second is the need to move on with life, to forget and adjust (Marris,

1974). Most Westerners tend to overlook the mourning and move on too quickly. There are, of course, many exceptions—some people never stop mourning. Many psychologists argue that both of these phases are necessary for healthy adjustment (Weisman, 1976).

Other changes present similar challenges. As individuals retire from work or later enter a retirement home, they must cope with the same problems of clinging to the past or denying the past and moving immediately into the future (Hughes, 1976). The same basic challenge of change may be found in educational transitions such as going from high school to college (Signell, 1976), moving to a new residence (Levine, 1976), and getting married (Rausch, Goodrich, and Campbell, 1976).

Deal (1985) provides current organizational examples portraying the same basic needs. At AT&T, for example, there were, and still are, many people who are bitter because of the need to give up the old service orientation and the halcyon days of the past.

I have met many managers who were almost frightened to allow people to express their sadness at the closing of a plant or a change in company orientation. They worried that expression of emotion would get out of hand or that people would hold out hopes for the revival of a plant or the old ways. Paradoxically, until employees are able to bury the past, the past seems to haunt them. In various subtle ways, people continue to live in the past and reminisce about the "good old days."

Many companies have sponsored ceremonies devoted to discussing feelings about the past. Sometimes these events have been informal gatherings where people could take pictures of the old group, reminisce about and eulogize the past, and, under the guise (or with the help) of inebriation, spout off about how they really feel. Other events have been formally organized with help from professionals who can facilitate, often in small groups, discussions of emotion.

These "mourning" events need to be handled carefully to ensure that everyone realizes that the past is really gone. Otherwise, the event becomes a chance for some people to lobby for and encourage false hopes. However, the sensitivity of such events suggests that they should be planned, not avoided.

Growing in New Ways

Let us now consider how an organization, or groups within it, can begin to grow in new directions and yet still not directly attack the whole company's character. The following six examples begin with the least obtrusive and end with the most obtrusive ways of moving to new practices and orientations.

1. *Allow things to grow in new ways:* Developing corporate character is similar to pruning trees. A gardener does not engineer a tree, but rather shapes and directs existing energy. This energy manifests itself in shoots that go in many directions. Essentially, the gardener decides what to let grow.

When attempting to redirect corporate character, we also need to think about letting things grow in alternative directions instead of dramatically altering a company's character. Indeed, perhaps the quickest way to begin reorienting character without destroying it is to look for opportunities to release pent-up energy and let people grow in ways they are already trying to grow.

For example, I was once asked to assist an organization in encouraging more concern for customer service. Upper-level management had spent five years introducing new budgetary procedures and efficiency measures to encourage cost cutting, but after a brief investigation I saw that existing staff members below middle management already had a great desire to serve clients in a sensitive and humane way. In fact, many told me that they were frustrated because they were unable to deliver the kind of service they would like.

In this case, the attempt to change focused on helping people find ways to achieve their pent-up desires. It was much more like allowing existing branches to grow toward the dominant energy source than hacking back limbs, or grafting on new branches, or forcing the growth toward the dark. The project met with tremendous emotional support. Within six months, the local community talked of how the company had turned around.

But the company turned around less than it headed in the direction that the existing staff was already facing. Recent years have brought even greater pressures for cost cutting to this company. However, management has learned that the competitiveness of its business and the commitment of its work force depend in great measure on the quality of its service. The managers continue to focus training time and executives' attention on improving service.

2. *Reward efforts in the right direction:* Welch at General Electric suggests another way to help organizations move in new directions. To compensate for strong management control systems and the cautious approach of the company, he has rewarded people for taking appropriate risks. Recently, when a $20 million project was scrapped because of a change in the market, Welch promoted the project manager and gave him a bonus. The seventy-member project team received videocassette recorders and bonuses instead of exile. Welch is not encouraging people to fail but to take reasonable risks even though the market or other forces outside of their control may later cause failure ("General Electric—Going with the Winners," 1984).

3. *Create punctuated evolution and reserves:* Some scholars in the field of biology (Eldrege and Gould, 1972) have proposed that evolution occurs in punctuated form, not in smooth and continuous changes. For example, instead of evolving one feather at a time, a duck makes a step-shift change (perhaps a mutation) and comes up with a rather complete new system (such as an abundance of feathers with oil on them) to compete and survive in a new environment.

This notion of punctuated evolution and step-shift change is instructive for companies. The recent experience at IBM with the personal computer provides a good organizational example. IBM executives became convinced that efforts to become competitive in personal computers were likely to be stifled within an institution that was accustomed to, and valued, the development of large systems for industrial customers. Therefore, they located a new division in Boca Raton away from headquarters, gathered people from inside and outside the company, and gave them significant freedom to do whatever they needed to make the personal computer division successful. These people, placed in isolation, began to violate some long-standing policies of IBM. For example, they decided to buy numerous computer components from suppliers rather than develop virtually everything themselves. They also realized that they would have to develop and invest significantly in new manufacturing technology. The result has been not a change in the overall IBM culture but a counterpoint—a very successful punctuated evolution that exemplifies some new ideas for the rest of the company.

Another *Fortune* 500 firm has recently created what executives call "reserves," places where new ideas and initiatives can be isolated and protected during development. Venture capital within the firm is offered to people who develop promising ideas that do not find ready acceptance within the current structure. Indeed, one such effort has been so successful following its allocation to reserve status that it now competes with the part of the business from which it was taken. Several managers have asked the president to return that business to them. He has refused, however, in order to encourage his employees to accept more new ideas and to see the consequences of not doing so. He also wants to visibly nurture these efforts as examples of alternative ways for the company to grow.

4. *Experiment:* Another alternative is to frame attempts to change as experimentation: a conscious effort to learn things, realizing that such efforts may not result in tremendous success.

Managers of Midland Mutual, a midwestern insurance company faced with significant earnings drops, discovered that they only knew one formula for doing business, the one that was no longer working. Rather than bet their company on one bold new strategy, they tried several small experiments in a variety of areas new for them. For example, they tried a joint venture with a large bank to use the bank's clientele and used direct mail to sell insurance. They also experimented with various new configurations of insurance and investment options. In addition, they allowed different groups within the company to experiment with self-generated ideas to improve service and reduce costs.

The president of this company, Gerald Mayer, told me that while several of the experiments had been successful, their major benefit was that people were coming alive to opportunities to improve. They no longer felt helpless about company dif-

ficulties. They worked for, and found, new ways to do their
work. But most importantly, they were learning how the business worked and how they could have an effect on it.

5. *Consider therapy:* If there is enough concern that the
company is in trouble, then executives may consider actions
that resemble therapy. For example, executives in one company
decided that their way of managing had become too bureaucratic. To stay competitive in their changing market required
greater innovation. Most of their early attempts at changing the
company were ill conceived and unsuccessful. They called in a
consultant to help them conduct an attitude survey. The survey's results helped them see that the top executives needed to
step away from the everyday business and reconsider the nature of their company and the relationships that managers had
with one another. The three top executives spent two days a
week for four months with the consultant off site and discussed
business books and considered observations gathered from within the company. They wanted to understand the basis of the
current management structure and relationships among people
in the company and to decide what company changes they
wanted and could realistically support. They later involved other vice presidents and their direct reports in their lengthy discussions, which resembled therapy in that they encouraged healthy
introspection and changed perspectives.

6. *Use selective surgery:* A more drastic process for
change might start with the perspective that some aspects of
the company need to be surgically removed. At General Electric, Welch has followed this strategy to some extent. He has
suggested that unless a part of his extensive conglomerate was a
strong factor in its business—number one or number two—it
probably did not belong in GE. Without "periodic pruning," as
he put it, "over the years you drag the whole business down to
a level, parceling out to the weak instead of infusing a winning
attitude in the whole." His intent has been to perform selective surgery—leaving the strong and active parts of the business
and cutting out some of the weaker parts ("General Electric—
Going with the Winners," 1984). Many people, of course, fear
surgery. They are afraid they could be cut next. But if execu-

tives consistently reward worthwhile efforts and build up the strong businesses, then that fear is attenuated.

One More Option: Revolution

Frequently executives may feel that they do not have much time to change their organization and that they must therefore turn to abrupt and drastic changes, or revolution. As I suggested in Chapter One, revolutions often successfully destroy certain aspects of the past without giving people something new to work with. Tragically, most companies that go through revolutions in leadership, in style, and in the type of markets they address are left without helpful precedent—without a usable past. Creating an entirely new history will, of necessity, take time. There is no alternative.

When a firm feels it must engage in revolution, its executives usually have been asleep at the controls. If they had allowed the organization to grow in new ways, rewarded efforts in the right direction, and encouraged continuous experimenting and learning how to learn, then they would have been much more responsive and able to change and apply their history to new situations. Hence, the need for a revolution is an indictment against current management. As we saw from the research by Dyer (1985), revolution almost invariably involves removing executives who have been asleep at the controls.

My observations of efforts to make significant organizational changes lead me to two general conclusions:

1. Before attempting significant organizational change, consider the costs of attacking current traditions directly and trying to destroy them. Roy Ash at Addressograph-Multigraph during the late 1970s and early 1980s was often cited as a take-charge guy or a charismatic leader. However, he was so willing to hack away at the basic roots of the company that he was soon deposed ("AM International . . . ," 1982).
2. Rather than trying to dismantle the old character, grow on the strengths of the past. Identify what has worked well previously and what will continue to work. In reality, there

is no alternative; people cannot simply cease to think and behave in old ways upon demand.

The best American executives have learned to add to our "Yankee can-do" attitude an appropriate sensitivity for the importance of past commitments, habits, and values. They encourage people to adapt and to understand the firm's new directions.

Honoring your past does not mean that you are trapped by the past. It does, however, suggest that you learn to bridge from past commitments and values to new ones. Where we cannot continue, we must learn to mourn the passing of cherished practices and orientations and then get on with life.

The next chapter considers how managers can build consensus about new directions through a process I call "negotiating a shared vision." While this chapter has focused largely on the *content* of the vision and its ability to bridge to the past, the next chapter emphasizes the *process* by which executives create and develop support for their vision of the future.

4

Negotiate a Shared Vision: Finding a Future That Fits

Perhaps few things are more dangerous to the well-being of organizational character than a high-sounding statement of a company's vision or management philosophy. Idealistic statements can raise employee hopes only to have them dashed when executives manuever the firm to survive in the face of unforeseen challenges. And the problem is worse if executives are initially successful in dramatizing the generation and publication of the statement so that many remember it.

As an example, recall the Canadian company mentioned in Chapter One where executives fashioned a statement of mission. Over the next few years the company suffered an increase of employee disillusionment because the company did not live up to the expectations the statement generated.

This case illustrates at least three critical challenges to the development of corporate character from the development of a clear statement of company vision or mission.

1. *It is invariably easier to say than to do:* The temptation to promise the moon increases when executives are in the spotlight and see their employees' hope for harmonious relations and superior performance. It is hard to resist comparing this phenomenon to New Year's resolutions. Who has not felt the swelling of hope and a sincere desire to do better when daily pressures are removed and the future offers apparently limitless possibilities? But in the case of vision statements, there is the

added motivation to be idealistic, which comes from the dreams of employees. If consulted, they will detail a company where all of their current problems are nonexistent.

The euphoria of "willing the future" by dreaming it makes the process of creating a statement of vision a potentially powerful tool to generate momentum and harmony in a company. Most writers about culture change therefore recommend developing some such statement, either of general management philosophy or of the hoped-for results of change, as an early step in the process of change.

However, the example of this Canadian company is typical. The future is so devilishly difficult to control and it is so easy to write down dreams for the future that employees and managers soon find disillusionment replacing dreams.

2. *Employees interpret the statement of philosophy from their own perspective and hopes:* Indeed, how else does someone understand the typically abstract and high-sounding values in vision statements?

Recall that in this Canadian company the statement suggested an increased emphasis on developing employee skills. However, executives at corporate headquarters intended a more centralized delivery of new development programs than did division managers. As a result, proposals for division-sponsored training were inevitably vetoed by corporate leaders, prompting criticism from divisions that the vision statement was empty rhetoric.

The strength of a statement of values or vision is that it is not precise and thus can capture the diverse hopes of many who might not agree on details but who can share general goals. Such a sharing of general values and hoped-for achievements—for example, producing the highest quality—can often motivate compromise as it lifts the group's aspirations.

However, the statement's very generality may also divide the group. Executives in one large consumer products company found that they could agree on wanting to be competitive in their industry and to deliver the highest-quality products and service. However, they could not agree on how to achieve those ends. Former IBM executives hired during a growth phase believed the problem should be solved by focusing on an IBM-like customer service orientation to improve products and service. But former Ford executives hired during the same period were equally convinced that the firm needed to work on better production standards and control. And each group pointed to the vision statement for justification.

3. *Some people will not accept the vision because it was "not invented here":* For some reason, they feel like Maleficent in the fairy tale of Sleeping Beauty. They were not invited or do not see their ideas fully included so they look for ways to criticize or even to sabotage the vision statement. When things go wrong they are quick to point out the lack of foresight in the statement.

In other words, for opponents vision statements are excellent vehicles for "I told you so" evaluations. Executives thus set themselves up for more visible failure the clearer and more public their vision statements are.

My intent is not to argue that executives should abandon vision or even that they should never publish a vision statement. Indeed, I have observed many companies where the statement of values mobilizes great energy and pride in the company. What I do hope to highlight is that such statements offer great potential challenges that must be understood and addressed.

Developing organizational character is a long-term and an ongoing process. What looks like the easiest aspect of change is often the most difficult. What appear to be early successes in gaining support for a new direction may turn out to be the sources of later failure. As a result, members of the organization must develop discipline to sustain long-term commitments that outlast the euphoria of announcing bold new visions. Employees are more likely to stay with long-term efforts if executives foster company-wide understanding of the process of mistake making and experimenting that lends integrity to sincere efforts.

Frankly, managing discipline and mistakes is simply less glamorous than creating vision. And few authors and consultants describe these more mundane management activities. Nevertheless, they are the stuff of organizational character development.

Of course, times of change may require that executives in

a firm explicitly reconsider the purpose and values they have followed sometimes implicitly. Many authors have suggested that managers engage in a formal process of "creating a mission statement," "creating a shared vision," or "writing a corporate philosophy statement." However, such formal processes tend to draw attention and create the idealistic expectations and misunderstandings just described. Therefore, because many executives will find it necessary to fashion a vision statement at some point, we should consider the relevant observations of several researchers and managers to learn what we can about how to address these challenges.

Research on corporate goal, mission, vision, or value statements lacks consensus. It offers a series of contradictory statements. I do not think that means the research is wrong, just that researchers described different situations or used different criteria and therefore came up with differing views. My plan in this chapter is to consider four areas of sometimes conflicting advice from researchers and popular business authors. Rather than resolve the conflicts, I want to suggest that the specific advice managers should take depends on their situation, their company's character, and their own risk preferences.

I have grouped conflicting counsel into four areas that are answers to the following questions:

1. Why is having a shared vision important?
2. What does vision look like? Is it the same thing as strategy or objectives?
3. Should we crystalize a shared vision as the first step in a change program or try to develop it as we go when we learn what we can really accomplish?
4. How can we develop shared vision?

Why a Shared Vision?

This is the area where there is least disagreement about vision. Basically, vision involves having people in the organization know the general purpose or role of their organization and, often in conjunction with a desired future state, the reasons why they should be proud of their organization. For example, Bata aims to be "shoemakers to the world," and IBM wants to be the best service organization in the world.

In this regard, four positive functions are most frequently mentioned as reasons for having a shared vision: inspiration, unobtrusive control, focus, and integration.

Inspiration. A shared vision can energize people by legitimizing the organization's existence (Kinston, 1986) and satisfying a basic human need: "the need to be important, to make a difference, to feel useful, to be part of a worthwhile enterprise" (Bennis and Nanus, 1985, p. 93). Without a widely shared vision, energy withers, apathy sets in, and the organization's vitality and productivity decline.

Firms that focus on maintaining good internal relationships, valuing employee development and rewarding performance, and having pride in their particular strengths and achievements tend to be higher performing than those that do not, according to a study by John Pearce and Fred David (1987) of a sample of *Fortune* 500 firms. Their study does not demonstrate causality, and some unsuccessful companies also mention these values in mission statements. Thus focusing on these values does not cause or ensure success. However, successful firms do tend to mention these values more often. Presumably, firms whose operating beliefs, as well as their mission statements, demonstrate real attention to these values more often benefit from the increased pride and motivation that such a focus can engender.

Unobtrusive Control. A shared vision may also provide an effective, yet unobtrusive, form of control of decisions. A shared vision may help to ensure that people will make decisions that are consistent with the organization's overall needs. Richard Pascale and Anthony Athos (1981) argue that because an executive cannot be everywhere at once, many decisions are made without his or her knowledge. A shared vision, in effect, provides employees with a compass that points their feet in the right direction. Of course, even if it were possible for the executive to be everywhere at once, close supervision may not be desirable because people often react against such obtrusive control. Indeed, William Ouchi (1981) argues that a widely shared philosophy can to some extent replace giving orders and closely supervising workers, thus leading to both increased productivity and supportive relationships at work. Shared vision can affect the perspective or premises that people use to make decisions and thus provide direction to control decisions in the absence of rules, direct supervision, or threats (Simon, 1945; Perrow, 1977).

Focus. A shared vision can channel the energy of the organization, preventing employees from dissipating their strengths in a variety of unrelated directions. Like the balloon you blew up as a child and let go, which hissed and darted and sputtered aimlessly, motivational faith without focus may produce movement but few useful results. Phillip Selznick (1957) points out that organizations without vision drift as they are exposed to short-run opportunistic trends. Because they lack focus, such organizations never develop a strong distinctive competence. By focusing individuals' attention on what is most important to the organization, visions help people uncover and eliminate a myriad of unproductive activities (McNeil, 1987).

Integration. A shared vision is also an integrating force in organizations, a mechanism for coordinating the efforts of groups with divergent interests. As John W. Gardner points out, shared visions can "lift people out of their petty preoccupations . . . and unify them in pursuit of objectives worthy of their best efforts. In the absence of some sense of purpose, energy is often wasted when political issues are repeatedly debated but never fully resolved" (in Berlew, 1974, p. 266). The absence of vision can result in endless struggles to influence where effort and resources should go (Kinston, 1986).

What Does a Vision Look Like?

A vision is usually not as concrete as measurable goals or objectives. It is not a specific strategy or tactic. Rather, it tends to be a broadly stated value (or values) that suggests a general focus and inspires, integrates, and controls organizational efforts. Selznick (1957) argues that the primary role of the leader who helps bring vision to the organization is to promote and protect values.

Vision must focus on values in addition to profit. Many employees do not value profit per se. Even those employees and managers who participate in profit sharing would find profit a rather opportunistic value that would not provide focus on certain skills or services; profit also would not always help to inspire and lift people beyond their self-interested biases.

Indeed, in an informal survey of company value statements, Terrence Deal and Allen Kennedy (1982) report that the most successful firms mentioned values other than profit, while the less successful focused almost entirely on profitability. It is not that successful firms ignore profits; indeed, in a recent and more rigorous study of a sample of *Fortune* 500 company mission statements, Pearce and David (1987) discovered that 90 percent of the firms explicitly mention that they value profitability. However, valuing profitability did not distinguish the top quartile performers from those in the bottom quartile. Rather, the top quartile firms more often stated additional values:

1. Human resource philosophies. For example, Sun Company says, "We believe human development to be the worthiest of the goals of civilization and independence to be the superior condition for nurturing growth in the capabilities of people." Mary Kay Cosmetics states, "The Mary Kay philosophy [is] a philosophy based on the golden rule. A spirit of sharing and caring where people give cheerfully of their time, knowledge, and experience."
2. Company self-concept or sense of competitive strengths. For example, "Hoover Universal is a diversified, multi-industry corporation with strong manufacturing capabilities, entrepreneurial policies, and individual businesses with autonomy" or "Crown Zellerbach is committed to leapfrogging competition within 1000 days by unleashing the constructive and creative abilities and energies of each of its employees."

3. Desired public image. Dow Chemical, for example, claims "to share the world's obligation for the protection of the environment," and Pfizer wants "to contribute to the economic strength of society and function as a good corporate citizen on a local, state, and national basis in all countries in which we do business" (1987, pp. 112–113).

Presumably these values, if given life through daily practices, systems, and top management attention, have the power to focus and inspire employees in ways that profit alone cannot. Speaking of similar organizations, Ouchi (1981, pp. 63–64) comments that "Among the fastest growing, most profitable of major American firms . . . profits are regarded not as an end in itself nor as the method of keeping score in the competitive process. Rather, profits are the reward to the firm if it continues to provide true value to its customers, to help its employees to grow, and to behave responsibly as a corporate citizen."

Indeed, some authors suggest that there are general values in America that are inspirational, if sincerely acted upon, to large groups of employees. For example, David Berlew (1974) says these three values are generally meaningful to many American employees: a chance to do something well, a chance to do something good, and a chance to change things. They suggest three different ways in which a vision can be formulated to mobilize the support of an organization's members.

A chance to do something well may be reflected in the vision of being the best, of valuing craft in a world of shoddy production. An example would be Northern Telecom's vision of living at the leading edge of technology.

A chance to do something good is reflected in the original vision at Matsushita: to advance the standard of living of the Japanese people by producing affordable and reliable electrical appliances. Other examples may involve the provision of worthwhile services or products, such as schooling, medical services, and counseling services, especially to the economically deprived. Hewlett-Packard's goal to be an economic, intellectual, and social asset to each nation and each community in which it operates could also qualify for many as doing something good.

A chance to change things is most often reflected in the visions of political and social movements. Whether it is to eliminate illiteracy, protect the environment, promote equality, or eradicate intolerance, a chance to change the way things are is a powerful source of excitement and energy in an organization. However, such visions are not restricted to political or social movements. One electronics company I have studied releases great energy by nurturing the vision that "we accomplish things that have never been done before, and we will revolutionize the way industry designs and tests its new products."

Just basing a company value statement on one or several of these values is no guarantee of employee motivation and support. Indeed, some companies may find that these values are not motivational given their particular history and employees' background. There are, however, certainly other values in addition to profit that can, if seriously implemented, capture the energy of specific groups of people. The executive task is to help discover and relate these values to the firm's activities.

Beyond the importance of values other than profit, the writing on shared vision suggests two additional concerns related to its content: (1) how idealistic or opportunistic it should be and (2) how precise and measurable or abstract and flexible it should be. Consider each of these controversies.

Between Idealism and Opportunism. The problem with trying to find idealistic values that are broad enough to inspire a large number of people is that they can become too idealistic and abstract to help in making tough choices. Indeed, Selznick (1957, p. 148) suggests two negative consequences that such "utopian abstraction" can create. He explains that the first occurs when people "who purport to be institutional leaders attempt to rely on overgeneralized purposes to guide their decisions. But when guides are unrealistic, yet decisions must be made, more realistic but uncontrolled criteria will somehow fill the gap. Immediate exigencies will dominate the actual choices." Ultimately, this means that the organization becomes a victim of its environment.

The second negative consequence of overly idealistic purposes is that people see little progress toward them. Hence, the lofty purposes result in discouragement rather than inspiration.

Peter Block (1987), however, takes a different point of view. He argues that a vision should be idealistic enough that people feel somewhat embarrassed and uncomfortable when they talk about it, as though it were almost religious. His point is that unless the vision is lofty and challenging, people do not stretch, and they fail to address the utmost of their potential and hopes.

My conclusion is that executives who take seriously the role of promoting and protecting important values should feel the tension between finding inspirational purposes that stretch and ennoble their employees and offering unrealistic goals. However, most managers I observe tend not to be too utopian. Rather, they want to quickly move to operating details and opportunities and tend to skip the underlying reasons and values. Managers can easily encourage opportunism that is too reactive to outside pressures and fails to take an aggressive stance toward defining and influencing their environment; as a result, the organization is allowed to drift with whatever the winds bring. The ill-fated efforts of RCA to diversify in the 1960s and 1970s can be attributed to opportunism. Its failure was in part due to being easily swayed by ephemeral trends (Dalton and Thompson, 1986).

Bradshaw, the CEO who was brought in to "clean up the mess" at RCA, explains: "The company had lost its way. . . . I guess other fields looked greener and it went into some ill-advised diversification efforts that didn't work out particularly well" (in Potts and Behr, 1987, p. 59). Perhaps opportunism is itself a form of utopianism. To think that one's organization can be all things to all people, or that it can be a master of all trades, is to be wildly unrealistic, if not utopian.

Can we be more precise about what is utopian and what is opportunistic? Perhaps, but not in ways that will be helpful to a given organization—because what is utopian and discouraging to some might not be so for others.

For example, Thomas Watson, Sr., had the vision of producing business machines that operate at the speed of light. In an absolute sense, that may be unrealistic, yet many in the organization saw progress in that direction as possible, and progress was made and will continue to be made. So too, Mahatma Gandhi's vision of an India free from intolerance must have appeared utopian to an extreme. However, although the goal was never achieved, visible progress was made. Visions that inspire often reflect an ideal that can only be approached but never fully attained. Service may be excellent today, but it has to be done all over again tomorrow.

Visions can be quite idealistic (like Gandhi's) yet still energize people. If leaders help people recognize incremental progress along the way and do not expect to arrive tomorrow, then people may not feel totally overwhelmed. In addition, if the vision does not fit the organization's existing competencies, then it must at least allow time for the organization to develop these competencies. People must believe that they have the ability to learn the new skills required.

We cannot therefore say from reading a statement of vision whether it is utopian or not. We need to understand it in the context of how an organization's members interpret, understand, and apply it.

Abstract and Flexible or Precise and Measurable? As executives attempt to develop a shared and motivating vision in their organization, they must consider how measurable to make their purposes. Shared visions may be very abstract—respect the dignity and rights of each employee (IBM)—or they may be quite precise—put a man on the moon by the end of the decade (John Kennedy). Nevertheless, even the vision of President Kennedy was such that it satisfied one of the conditions Ouchi (1981, p. 121) stressed: It can "be applied to each of the activities of the company, from research to manufacturing, selling, and even the mail clerk."

While some theorists suggest that a firm's goals should be precise and measurable, others have contradicted these hallmarks of professional management. For example, Edward Wrapp (1967) and James Bryant Quinn (1977) found that successful executives rarely announced quantitative or measurable goals. Most often goals were stated in very broad and general terms. Similarly, Gene Dalton and Paul Thompson (1986) argue that a "commonly held map" or shared vision helps people explain what the firm is doing in the face of surprises, partly because it is ambiguous and general enough to accommodate new events. Very specific goals do not allow people to find meaning in a changing world.

Although the general rule is for visions to be broad and general, there are times when a specific objective is needed. No one can discount the energizing effect that NASA's vision, announced by President Kennedy in 1960, had on NASA. The vision of "putting a man on the moon by the end of the decade" provided for more focus, direction, collaboration, and energy than could have been achieved with a statement such as "We are going to be on the leading edge of space exploration." One of the critical roles of a leader, then, is to determine when commitment to a concrete objective is not only helpful but also badly needed (Dalton and Thompson, 1986).

Quinn (1977), who has strongly argued that successful executives rarely announce specific goals, recognizes that sometimes specific goals can be very functional. Quinn identifies three conditions when announcing specific goals can benefit an organization: (1) the goal is clearly realistic, (2) key people in the organization already understand and support it, and (3) the executive establishes a completion date that is sufficiently distant to allow for flexibility in case of unforeseen developments and obstacles.

Although shared visions must help people cope with reality, they can never be expected to mirror reality precisely. As Thomas Sowell (1987, p. 79) cautions: "Reality is far too complex to be comprehended by a given mind. Visions are like maps that guide us through a tangle of bewildering complexities. Since visions have to do with an unpredictable future, common sense should warn us that they can never hope to mirror reality precisely."

Although successful visions are not designed to mirror reality, they do need to be anchored in reality. A vision that takes no account of the environment, or ignores the capabilities of the organization, is courting disaster.

AM International, referred to in Chapter One, provides an excellent example of the problems that follow initially shared but unanchored visions. Its vision was to revitalize an aging office equipment line of products by turning to high technology. Managers bought high-technology companies and brought in new managers to run them. But they did not ensure that the new factories could produce reliable, high-precision products. They also overlooked weaknesses in the ability of existing field operators to sell and service the new products. Such capacity, called "execution skill" in Chapter One, must be grown; it cannot be imported (see Hayes, 1986).

Should the Shared Vision Come First or Later?

Many who write about cultural change suggest that developing a shared mission or vision is the first step. They argue that major organizational change should be guided by some sense of new direction and hope. Indeed, Richard Beckhard and Reuben Harris (1987) argue that the vision of the future should be as precise and detailed as possible, with measurable benchmarks along the way to guide the metamorphosis.

Harry Levinson and Stuart Rosenthal (1984) suggest just the opposite in their study of six successful CEOs. They report that none of the CEOs they studied started with a clearly articulated vision. At GE, for example, two years passed before Reginald Jones articulated his vision for the organization, and he had been with GE almost all his working life.

Perhaps the resolution of these contradictions comes in considering the differences in conditions facing firms that start with the announcement of a clear and new vision and those that evolve such a vision after experimenting and perhaps building support behind the scenes.

There are times when a leader can enter an organization from the outside and transform it within a fairly short time. This usually occurs when an organization is in crisis and most of its members acknowledge that the old visions and norms clearly are not working. In the face of the organization's possible demise, people are willing to give the new leader a lot of latitude, at least in the short term (Gabarro, 1985). If the organization then moves into a more healthy and stable state, and if the change for the better is attributed to the new leader and his vision, then employees will usually come to support the new vision and the values it embodies (Dyer, 1985).

Crisis not only provides the leader with a license to dictate a new vision but it also, as Quinn (1977) notes, may make such behavior both functional and necessary. After a prolonged crisis or deep trauma, clear new goals can give people new hope and direction to help them make necessary transitions. New maps, as Dalton and Thompson (1986, p. 141) explain, are critical because "it is easier to give up an old map if you have a new one with which to replace it." Even when old maps are not working, people are often reluctant to discard them unless they have something to take their place.

The "advantage" of crisis, however, does not guarantee success. If the organization does not begin to improve following the announcement of a new vision, it is unlikely that the vision will receive long-term support. Although crisis may reduce the leader's dependency on specific knowledge about the company that is usually needed to win support for the new vision, I argue that success depends on how well the vision is anchored to the competencies of the organization and the reality of its environment. This explains why most of those who succeed in transforming organizations even in times of crisis at least come from the same industry if not from the company itself.

Indeed, Thomas Peters and Robert Waterman (1982) note that most of the leaders of their "excellent" companies grew up in the business. The same applied to eight of the nine leaders Levinson and Rosenthal (1984) discuss. Mark Potts and Peter Behr (1987, p. 200) studied ten highly successful CEOs and concluded that "they tend to be hands-on managers who have risen from the ranks—more knowledgeable about their companies than many CEOs of the past." All three of the transforming college presidents described by Burton Clark (1970) grew up in the business of education. Although being a transforming leader is not totally restricted to those who grow up in the business, transforming leaders who come in from the outside need to be able to learn very fast.

Except when crisis makes organizational members willing to forgo usual differences in values to help the organization survive, executives should work at evolving support for new visions. This notion is somewhat counterintuitive. Should not leaders provide vision to guide their organizations?

I present below a summary of descriptions by several authors who describe this often more normal and successful evolutionary approach to creating vision. Following this description of the overall process, we will then consider how leaders help create a shared vision through evolution by (1) listening to and learning from others, (2) inspiring confidence, (3) acting out the vision before announcing it, and (4) exercising power on behalf of organizational interests and using persuasive and informal power before formal sanctions. These actions by leaders make it more likely that a vision will be internalized and that organizational participants will learn to engage in continual renewal of the vision.

Creating a Shared Vision: The Process

The incremental process leaders use in negotiating a shared vision does not appear to be much different from what Quinn (1980) describes as the process that successful executives follow as they formulate new strategies. Indeed, many such executives will experiment with strategy and use that experience to fashion a broad vision. Rather than quickly locking themselves into irreversible commitments, creating undesired centralization, or providing a focus for opposition, successful executives follow a process of "logical incrementalism"—an evolutionary, experimental, largely political process for building consensus—according to Quinn. This process is advocated not only for political reasons but also, as Quinn correctly points out, it is often the sole way executives can make informed decisions in environments of uncertainty. Only an incremental process will allow for testing, feedback, and flexible revision based on the new information the process produces. In this way the strategy tends to evolve as internal decisions and external events come together (Quinn, 1980).

This process of incrementalism is essential to avoid what

Selznick calls "premature self-definition." Although transforming leaders are bound to consult the values of their constituents,
they must first determine which values are truly unalterable.

An incremental process for refining the vision allows leaders to separate the "weakly held and readily altered" opinions
from "true self-defining commitments of external and internal
constituents" (Selznick, 1957, p. 69). Quinn (1977, p. 14)
quotes the president of a company who describes the very process Selznick recommends:

> We are a very large company, and we understand
> that any massive overt action on our part could
> easily create more public antagonism than support
> for our viewpoint. It is also hard to say in advance
> exactly what public response any particular action
> might create. So we tend to test a number of dif-
> ferent approaches on a small scale with only lim-
> ited or local company identification. If one ap-
> proach works, we'll test it further and amplify its
> use. If another bombs, we try to keep it from being
> used again. Slowly we find a series of advertising,
> public relations, and community relations actions
> that seem to help. Then along comes another issue
> and we start all over again. Gradually the successful
> approaches merge in a pattern of actions that be-
> comes our strategy.

When General Rawlings became president of General
Mills, he followed an even more political, though incremental
and unobtrusive, process to avoid opposition from internal constituents. He developed a Corporate Analysis Department,
which made informal presentations to top management on a
variety of issues. Within time, these reviews became formal
presentations to which all corporate and divisional top managers and controllers were invited. Problem operations were
studied in depth. Soon attention began to focus on a number of
acquisitions made after World War II. Two unprofitable acquisitions—the formula feeds business (cattle mix) and the low-profit

electronics business—were sold. It was not until after these moves that official statements of the president suggested management was focusing on major strengths. Only then was management able to tackle head on a reconsideration and eventual divestiture of the company's traditional core business of flour milling (Quinn, 1980).

The power Rawlings exercised lay in his ability to reinterpret history, to ask key questions, to set the agenda for his staff department, to make presentations to top management, and to select those attending certain meetings.

Note also that General Mills started divesting businesses in those areas it felt would create the least opposition. Also note that only once the organization was already moving in the new direction did its leader start to openly articulate the new vision.

Establishing task forces and blue-ribbon committees, releasing trial balloons, deliberately leaking information, canvassing trusted colleagues, negotiating individually with key people, developing informal networks, cultivating common ground, and strategically waiting for the right moment are all ways to incrementally negotiate a new vision, building support along the way. Only after enough key people are on board does the transforming leader announce the new vision, reinterpreting history to show how past decisions, actions, and events have already given momentum to this new direction.

As we have already discussed, establishing a vision also requires the leader to take account of the environment. Once again, an incremental process is one of the most effective ways to make sense of it. As Selznick (1957) points out, leaders must both be aware of pressures from the environment and avoid the surrender of character in the name of organizational survival. For example, a public university president may take into account the demands of the state legislature or special-interest groups without allowing them to determine university policy. The leader must seek allies, find alternate sources of funding, and try to understand the seriousness of external threats as ways of creating the means and the will to withstand environmental pressures. In other words, although leaders need to consult the environment and the organization's members before crystalizing a vision, they must not allow these forces to dictate the vision. With this introduction to incrementalism, we are ready to consider specific leadership actions that encourage the evolution of a shared vision.

1. *Listening to develop a shared vision:* Developing a shared vision begins with communication—but not the communication of speeches and political conventions. When talking of transforming leaders, we immediately think of those leaders with extraordinary verbal skills: Winston Churchill, Franklin Roosevelt, or Abraham Lincoln. However, in their study of sixty successful CEOs, Warren Bennis and Burt Nanus (1985) found that speaking ability was not a prerequisite for creating a shared vision—but listening was.

Although the ability to persuade is an important part of transforming leadership, listening appears to be at the core of this persuasive process. The reason is simple. Certain leaders may be the first to openly advocate the vision, but usually "the vision did not originate with the leaders personally but rather from others . . . the leader only rarely was the one who conceived of the vision in the first place. . . . Successful leaders, we have found, are great askers, and they do pay attention" (Bennis and Nanus, 1985, p. 96).

This view that most leaders do not get their visions from some mysterious inner resource is supported in both political and anthropological literature. James McGregor Burns (1978) points out that leadership in political settings occurs when someone is able to mobilize others in ways that engage, arouse, and satisfy their needs. Thus, leadership is inseparable from the needs of followers (see also Berlew, 1974). For example, Burns argues that the true genius of Mao Tse-tung was his understanding of others' emotions. The needs, goals, or emotions of other people should therefore play a crucial role in shaping the vision that the leaders formulate within their own mind.

John Gillan (1948), an anthropologist, points out that cultures change when individuals can articulate a need that most people in society have vaguely felt but have not explicitly recognized. In contrast to this view, Anthony Wallace (1956, p. 270) argues that new vision in "revitalization movements" seems normally to occur in "the mind of a single person rather than to grow directly out of group deliberations" (p. 270). However, he does note that "The original doctrine is continuously modified by the prophet, who responds to various criticisms and affirmations by adding to, emphasizing, playing down, and eliminating selected elements of the original visions. This reworking makes the new doctrine more acceptable to special-interest groups, may give it a better fit to the population's cultural and personality patterns, and may take account of the changes occurring in the general milieu" (1956, pp. 274–275).

Thus Wallace's view enriches and is consistent with Gillan's view. Although a new vision may find its first articulated form in the mind of a single person, the original subcomponents and later elaborations of that form usually come from others. These subcomponents and elaborations may not grow directly out of the "group deliberations" that Wallace refers to, but they do emerge from a group process—even if it is not a formal or deliberate one.

Thomas Peters and Nancy Austin (1985) argue that the creation of vision does not come from group process techniques but that it starts with a single individual. They claim that "the raw material of the effective vision is invariably the result of one man's or woman's soul-searching" (1985, p. 286). I would argue that soul-searching is not enough. Soul-searching is obviously necessary so that the leader will feel the utmost commitment to the vision. However, the vision also needs to be grounded in reality and in the values and needs of the followers. If leaders are not sensitive to their followers' aspirations, fears, and values, then they will never have the essential elements from which to fashion shared vision. Although these elements may take on their reconstituted form in the mind of a single individual, they seldom originate with the leader.

2. *Inspiring confidence:* A critical tool for charismatic leaders is the ability to inspire people with confidence. David McClelland (1975, p. 258) found that people who were exposed to a charismatic leader "were apparently strengthened and uplifted by the experience; they felt more powerful, rather than

less powerful and submissive. . . . He does not force them to submit and follow him by sheer overwhelming magic of his personality and persuasive powers. . . . In fact, he is influential by strengthening and inspiring his audience. . . . The leader arouses confidence in his followers. The followers feel better able to accomplish whatever goals he and they share." Strengthening and inspiring people may occasionally require great speaking skills. When one is appealing to a mass audience, these skills are probably essential. But in modern organizations, these skills are neither essential nor sufficient, although they would definitely be an asset. Communicating confidence and a feeling of progress can be done in many ways besides grand speeches. In the long run, action, not words, sustains confidence and energy.

In her book on charismatic political leadership, Ann Wilner (1984) describes how Franklin Roosevelt changed the atmosphere in Washington, D.C., from one of despair to one of hope. Although his rhetoric had something to do with this change, his actions may have been even more important. Wilner suggests that while the major economic impact of his actions would not be felt for years, the psychological impact was "bracing and revivifying."

Of Winston Churchill, Art McNeil (1987, p. 45) writes, "He [recognized] that every public act was an opportunity to send a powerful signal. . . . He converted every public act into a microcosm of his nation's will to resist. He carried on with his personal duties in London during the blitz, making no concessions to danger, accepting the same conditions as the general public, demonstrating at every opportunity that he would not run from the enemy."

Successful leaders need to be totally committed to their visions. If they want their people to sacrifice for the vision, then they need to be willing to lead by example. Iacocca's "one dollar a year" salary reflected this type of commitment. By contrast, the $1 million annual salary of Archibald McCardle at International Harvester made his demand that union members take salary cuts to help save the company particularly unpalatable. The following bitter strike led to McCardle's ouster and to serious damage to the company.

To sustain energy, commitment, and confidence, transforming leaders also look for opportunities to celebrate "small wins" (Peters and Waterman, 1982). They recognize the need to encourage people through their actions as well as their words. Transforming leaders do not use "management by wandering around" as a way to check up on people. They use it as an opportunity to keep in touch, to listen, to signal the vision, and to give individuals encouragement and help. A senior Bell Labs manager quoted by Peters and Austin (1985, pp. 391–392) describes what encouragement and help look like:

> My job? Run the Xerox machine for a team at three A.M. the morning their project is due for review. I spend half my time just asking dumb questions: "What's bugging you?" "What's getting in the way?" It turns out it's seldom big stuff. It's usually petty annoyances. A small group needed a personal computer, and was being dragged through an almost full-blown capital budget review to get one. I got them one in forty-eight hours. And so on. Running interference and kicking down small hurdles. Nobody will come to you with this stuff. They think it's "too trivial" to bother you with! They think they ought to be able to do it themselves. So they'll tie themselves up in knots for a week on some little nit.

As Peters and Waterman (1982) suggested, successful companies realize that success comes from harnessing the energy of almost everyone in the organization—not just the top 10 percent. Consequently, companies like IBM try to ensure that 80 percent of their sales force achieve membership in the Hundred Percent Club. Although the top 3 percent do get special recognition as members of the Golden Circle, the majority of the salespeople still feel competent. Leaders in these companies apparently do not wait for excellent performance before they start celebrating and rewarding it. They look for and celebrate even moderately good performance, recognizing that each step in the right direction brings them marginally closer to realizing their vision.

3. *Acting before announcing:* Although Bennis and

Nanus (1985) did not find great rhetoric to be a distinguishing characteristic of all their CEOs, "signaling" certainly was. Leaders signal through their actions, both big and small, what the vision is, how it can be attained, and what progress is being made.

McNeil (1987) argues that actions should precede any grand announcements of a new vision. Only after the leader has "lived" the vision for a time does it make sense to publicize it. There may be occasions when leaders can maximize their impact by making grand announcements, but more often than not grand announcements provide a focus for opposition. Such announcements may also create cynicism if the leader later feels unable or unwilling to live the vision.

Because it is not easy to always send consistent signals, even when one strongly believes in them, living them first is the best way for a leader to share the vision while at the same time learning to be consistent. Then when the announcements are made, cynicism is less likely to be the harvest. Making the signaling process habitually consistent is also critical preparation for times when circumstances place a great deal of pressure on the leader. When the leader's mind is preoccupied with numerous urgent problems demanding undivided attention, he or she is then able to provide consistent responses almost instinctively. Responses during crisis become the acid test of a leader's commitment to the vision (Schein, 1983). For example, the actions of Johnson & Johnson executives during the crisis created by tampering with Tylenol bottles demonstrated a serious concern for consumers that was impressive. While the company must have lost significant profits in the short run by recalling the product, developing "tamper-proof" bottles, and setting up answering services for customer questions, in the long run its reputation has been strengthened, and its market share has returned. Actions like these, not speeches or slogans, build trust and commitment.

Although managers could see challenges as a nuisance or a threat, a leader sees them as an opportunity to signal. Major challenges often provide a leader with great visibility. By responding consistently in such cases, the leader is assured that such signals will have the greatest possible impact on the greatest number of people. In turn, if the leader behaves consistently, he or she will be more likely to earn the trust and faith of others.

Given the dangers of "announcementitis," such a leader usually starts by signaling in small ways. This allows the leader time to discover what works and what does not. The leader can then adjust the vision without being seen as inconsistent or selling out. Only when such leaders know what is possible and what people value do they worry about making speeches, producing mission statements, and hanging up plaques that articulate the vision.

4. *Exercising power in support of the vision:* Although transforming leaders concentrate on highlighting and rewarding the positive, they are not afraid to show disapproval—be it through firing individuals, demoting them, or publicly reprimanding them. Levinson and Rosenthal (1984, p. 269) argue that "This last quality, a form of aggression, is not touched on in most of the contemporary discussions of leadership. Yet we found it an important part of the leader's role. If one is to hold up an ideal, then one must also reject that behavior which compromises the ideal. It is not enough to merely hold it up."

Although not afraid to take action against those who refuse to support new visions, transforming leaders do not use their formal power lightly. Levinson and Rosenthal (1984) note that the leaders in their study emphasized persuasion rather than edict and sought to obtain commitment rather than compliance. Transforming leaders appear to recognize that too much reliance on formal power not only reflects poor leadership and an admission of failure but also can erode rather than enhance leaders' credibility and informal power (Neustadt, 1980). Reliance on formal power can destroy the often fragile trust that is at the core of all cooperative human endeavors.

Then how do executives deal with people who are unwilling or unable to support the new vision, while avoiding alienating a large part of the organization? Although successful leaders of change will praise specific people publicly, they usually restrict public reprimands to behaviors rather than people. Only when a person blatantly violates a commonly held value (for example, by being dishonest), or when noncompliance is so widely known that inaction will call into question the leader's commitment to the vision, will the transforming leader resort to formal power. As long as people believe this formal power is being exercised in the organization's best interests, and not for personal ends, the leader will preserve power in the organization and may even enhance it. The findings of Dalton and Thompson (1986, p. 169) support this: "To the extent that those empowered to act for the organization wink at abuses, they lose power. To the extent that they act to stop or prevent abuses to the point where others feel that they can trust the integrity of the system, these individuals gain power."

Learning to exercise power is one of the most challenging tasks of leadership. Although a leader in an organization enjoys formal power, much of what he or she does depends on the willingness of others to cooperate—their willingness to entrust the leader with informal power (Dalton and Thompson, 1986). Ultimately, the only power a leader truly has is the power to persuade (Neustadt, 1980). Although formal command is one method of persuasion, it is "not a substitute, and not a method suitable for everyday employment. . . . To unsheathe the sword of formal commands before it is necessary and without it being a part of a web of other forms of persuasion is to lose power" (Dalton and Thompson, 1986, p. 177).

Although leaders must challenge and remove behaviors or people threatening the vision, they apparently try to sell their visions rather than impose them. As I argued in Chapter Three, instead of dwelling on "pruning" the system of undesirable behaviors and values, leaders encourage the desirable. Over time, the undesirable characteristics are often crowded out by the desirable. To change my metaphor, one can cure certain diseases by surgically removing the diseased tissue, or one can build up the body's immunity system to fight the disease. Leaders concentrate on the second approach, although they do not shrink from surgery when they consider it necessary to remove a limb to save a life.

Finally, the key to building persuasive power lies not in the acquisition of power for its own sake, but in investing what power one has in people and activities that further the interests of the organization. The quickest way to lose the power to persuade is to use one's power purely for self-interested ends. Ronald Reagan's highly proclaimed ability to persuade, at least during the first six years of his presidency, came from his consistency, persistence, and ability to show others how what he wanted them to do was in the country's best interests. However, it does not take a keen observer to note how fast some of this power evaporated in the wake of the Iran-Contra affair. When the Iran-Contra affair cast doubt on Reagan's consistency, integrity, and the nature of the interests he used his powers to serve, some people withdrew their willingness to be persuaded. The power to persuade, like any other form of power, is exercised with the permission of those who are the objects of that persuasion.

Earning the Right to Announce Vision

Shared vision is the product of organizational effort, not the announcement of a management committee. It is most effective if it results from the successful efforts of many organizational experiments. Just as we might prefer that an individual develop strong character traits and earn, rather than merely ask for, our respect, organizations need to earn the right to announce the values they stand for. Indeed, I have been working for some time with a plant management team that decided more than a year ago not to post and celebrate the company's new mission statement. They were sure employees in the plant would be cynical about the pronouncements concerning quality products and the quality of work life. They have done a great deal of soul-searching and made significant personal changes in preparation for establishing and modeling operating beliefs in their plant.

Shared vision statements are best when they capture ongoing truths about the organization and when they represent the values and needs of employees as well as the real competitive challenges of the organization. When executives listen carefully to the needs and values of employees, inspire confidence, act before they announce, and, finally, use their power (particularly their power to persuade) to support emerging vision, they are most likely to help their organizations to develop a shared vision. The only exceptions to these general principles seem to occur during times of crisis. And even in those situations visions must correspond to organizational realities and competencies.

Fleshing out the vision for the organization includes doing more of the same. In the next chapter I focus on some critical and concrete details to which managers should attend if vision is to become reality.

5

Implement the Vision:
Making the Dream Real

With the dawning of the 1980s, executives and managers of Esso Chemicals of Canada were agreed that their business had changed fundamentally and that they would have to use a very different strategy to survive. The previous sellers' market had become crowded with an increased number of domestic and international competitors that were supplying petrochemicals.

Company executives had taken close to a year to develop a clear vision of how their company should respond. They came to agree that in addition to becoming the low-cost supplier of basic products, they should also develop niche-oriented products through joint ventures and joint-development agreements with customers. The new strategy meant faster, more flexible production and new relationships with customers. Both thrusts were significant departures for the company, but appeared to be critical for survival.

After several months, top managers began to wonder why very little had changed. What went wrong? As they later discovered, while employees agreed with the general ideas, they were unsure whether top managers were really serious about the new

Note: I am indebted to Jon Younger, currently of Novations Group, Inc., for this account. He served as internal organizational development consultant during this period and helped devise many of the processes used to facilitate the development of character.

thrusts and did not know what they specifically needed to do differently. Middle management saw a number of historical inconsistencies among the strategy, the organizational rewards, and management behavior.

Top management discovered these problems by meeting with groups of twelve to fifteen employees at all levels throughout the company to get their input. These executives heard firsthand about employees' concerns across the organization. For example, some managers complained that executives said they wanted more risk taking and development of new products, but would not approve the building of new tanks (in which to develop new products) without precise justification of the new sales.

Achieving agreement about a new vision or strategy may be the easiest step in developing new organizational character. Unless top management backs up its exhortations to operate differently with changed personal behavior that exemplifies the new thrust and demonstrates the priorities of new values and practices over old ones, employees will often treat their pronouncements as so much rhetoric and grow cynical about the prospects of change.

Managers at Esso also expressed confusion about the specifics of implementing the new strategy. They complained that many of the organization's "rules" got in the way. Internal organizational development consultants had them list these rules in small group interviews. Fully 60 percent of what employees listed as constraints to change were informal customs or practices, social conventions, the habits of the organization. Most of these conventions were not written down anywhere; they were what some employees had learned about the best way to get things done and had passed on to other employees.

Some of the conventions were directly counter to the new strategic thrust. For example, many in the organization believed that it was an iron-clad rule that managers should not give more than a gallon of product to the customer. Of course, customers need much more than a gallon of crude oil in jointly developing new products. In 1975 an internal audit team had concluded that the company was giving too much product to customers. The sales manager had felt personally criticized and passed his conclusion along: "If you know what's good for you, don't give more than a gallon of product to the customer." Many other conventions also directly conflicted with the new strategy.

It takes time to experiment with new practices and for the grapevine to report on successes, failures, and improvements. It takes a myriad of such conventions to equip a large and complex organization with enough skill and flexibility to make organizational responses predictable, appropriate, and of high quality. It takes even more time for the effects of these new and improved organizational practices to impress customers and suppliers so that the organization develops a new role, or reputation, with these groups.

In summary, significant changes in organizational vision and strategy require significant changes in both the formal systems and the informal conventions if the organization is to develop competitive execution skills. Esso Chemicals' managers learned that they must do much more than develop a shared vision about needed changes. Their experience suggests that managers must also (1) demonstrate through changes in their own behavior the priority of new values and how these new values can be practiced and (2) create an administrative system with supporting incentives and developmental experiences to foster new execution skills in the organization. We will consider each of these executive tasks in turn.

Demonstrating the Priority and Practice of New Values

John Akitt, president of Esso Chemicals, was quick to respond to questions from managers about how serious he was about the new directions. He made several immediate changes:

1. He personally championed customer visits by asking customers how Esso could improve products and services and by encouraging others to do the same.

2. He led a comprehensive strategy reappraisal of each of the businesses to determine how each could better implement the new directions.
3. He instituted a monthly lunch, meeting with different groups throughout the company to respond to their questions and share his enthusiasm and vision.
4. He encouraged groups within the company to operationalize for themselves how they could implement a customer focus specifically.
5. The previous year had seen a number of layoffs due to declining business. He had the name of each employee put on his or her office door, a symbolic move that buttressed his message that this was a team he expected to work with to achieve their shared vision.

People saw Akitt identify the previous organizational inconsistencies and respond to feedback and change. The effect was dramatic. Many managers and employees felt able to make needed corrections as well. They were also given some important signals from Akitt's actions about where they should spend their time and what he considered the organization's new priorities. They began to tell one another stories about his actions that clarified and gave credence to the company's new thrusts.

Executives next met with managers in small groups throughout the organization to "peel the onion." They had employees list all the conventions that seemed to be counter to the new direction and talked about them. Together with managers, they tried to come up with sensible changes in these informal operating rules.

The result of these meetings was that managers gained a much clearer sense of what executives had in mind about implementing the new strategy. But more importantly, they were able to improvise and find ways to deliver on organizational promises. Initial efforts were not always correct, but they learned and improved quickly. In the process they developed a commitment and a sense of pride about executing the new vision (Dalton, 1970).

Three years later, these executives at Esso Chemicals felt

they had made significant progress. They were convinced, however, that they still needed to improve relative to two competitors who had been working longer on customizing products for,
and developing new products with, customers.

My research in organizations suggests that many of the
values that are adopted as shared vision, as well as the conventions people learn, are passed on through informal stories (Wilkins, 1983b). Stories of actual events inside the organization are
often more credible than official claims because the person who
is telling the story may not be a company official (with obvious
pro-company biases) and because the story is concrete, unlike
the abstract ideas of vision statements. In addition, stories give
people a chance to improvise their own implementation of orga-
nization-sponsored values.

When managers hear about the importance of informally
told stories in passing on and clarifying critical values and practices, they often ask how they can influence stories. My response
is that such stories arise from actions they and others take that
are consistent (or inconsistent) with espoused values. They have
the greatest positive influence on informal accounts when they
have a clear vision about where the company should be going,
when their daily behavior—where they spend their time, what
they reward or question—is consistent with the vision, and when
they take advantage of certain tense situations to make a dramatic statement with their actions. In general, the popular
stories I observe in organizations derive from dramatic management actions—those that occur during a time of crisis or are out
of the ordinary. Other actions seem to be taken for granted and
slide into oblivion.

Beyond the congruence and timing of executive action,
stories become popular when they relate to the needs and hopes
of organizational members. Hence, executives attuned to the
concerns and expectations of people in their organization can
direct their actions to dramatically influence what people talk
about.

I suggest below some ways managers can think about dramatizing their beliefs. I also offer some advice about how managers can use their daily activities to support the vision of the

organization. My advice may be summarized as a prescription for managers to both pounce on opportunities to dramatize the vision and to practice what they preach. (Many of the examples used throughout the remainder of this chapter were taken from Wilkins, 1984.)

Pouncing on Opportunities to Demonstrate Values. A group of managing partners of a financial services firm was concerned about the stories that would be told following the promotion of Dave to a partner in the firm. Since Dave had not worked in sales, this was an unprecedented event in the organization, and the managers were sure it would create a stir. The new partner would receive significant ownership opportunities not normally available to staff people. Partners were concerned that the promotion would perhaps give license to other staff people in the organization to neglect some mundane aspects of their jobs and focus on the more visible things Dave had done. Dave had been unusual in his ability to help partners develop new products that had made a lot of money for the firm. He was also very proficient in the mundane aspects of his job. These partners did not know if other staff people were aware of how responsible and skillful Dave had been at both. They were also quite sure that very few, if any, of the other staff members would have the ability to become a partner. Hence, they wanted to communicate that promoting this new staff person to partner was unusual. They wished to convey several other messages, and they sought my advice about how to convey clearly all of these messages throughout the organization.

It is very difficult to deliver any clear messages throughout an organization, let alone a complex message such as they sought to deliver. My counsel was that this group seek to make one bold and simple statement to the organization: that Dave was an unusual person who had done a variety of things well and therefore was clearly deserving. On a subsequent occasion, if they discovered that people were indeed ignoring their mundane responsibilities, they could pounce on that opportunity to teach.

If managers will be content to teach clearly one idea at a

time, then they are likely to develop much greater complexity of understanding in their organizations. To illustrate how pouncing can dramatize key values, let me offer some examples of actions that have become stories in companies.

One example comes from a new plant where managers and employees had spent significant time discussing their desire to foster creativity, productivity, trust, and openness. Before the plant opened, managers and employees had met to jointly compose a statement of principles to guide their relationship. One of the most important of these principles was that employees and management would trust one another and treat each other as partners in the plant. One way they chose to symbolize this was by establishing an open cash box. Anyone could put in an IOU and borrow cash and then pay the box back within some time period.

When the plant manager arrived at work one morning, the whole plant was abuzz. He discovered that everyone was talking about the fact that someone had taken $60 from the cash box without leaving an IOU. Several employees were predicting that this would be the beginning of the end for the new trust policy. Three managers held a quick meeting and then called the employees together. The plant manager said he was sorry the money was gone and hoped it would be returned. He did not want to overreact; perhaps someone had just forgotten to leave an IOU. He also pulled $10 out of his own pocket and said he personally wanted to contribute to replenishing the cash box. Several others quickly followed suit, and the trust policy was given a clear symbol. Everyone used the story to say, in a way that abstract philosophizing could not, that the management gave employees a fair chance and that the idea of trust was alive at the plant.

As this example illustrates, stories are particularly likely to form during periods of crisis when clear and imaginative action is taken.

Another dramatic action in the name of values during a crisis comes from Hewlett-Packard. Perhaps the most widely known story at HP, at least during the late 1970s, is about how the company avoided a mass layoff in the early 1970s when almost every company in the industry was forced to lay off employees in large numbers. Top management at HP discovered that there had been a serious drop in orders, which had affected the entire industry and resulted in HP being 10 percent short in its cash to meet payroll.

The top managers felt committed to their value of teamwork ("we share together in the good times and in the bad") and their value of long-term employment. This was an opportunity to demonstrate the depth of their commitment. They asked everyone in the company, themselves included, to take a 10 percent cut in salary and come to work only nine out of ten days. They also instituted a program wherein employees from the hardest-hit divisions were transferred to other divisions. People were given make-work like painting the factory and cleaning up so that they did not produce goods for inventory that could not be sold.

This experience became known as the "nine-day fortnight" and has been a very popular story in the company. Employees often use it as a symbol to communicate the idea that HP is a "company with a heart."

A final example of pouncing suggests that pouncing can create a sense of drama in even mundane encounters. At Hewlett-Packard the practice is to call people by their first names. As the story goes, a recently hired young man is sent to deliver something to Bill Hewlett. When he arrives at the office, he begins by addressing Bill as "Mr. Hewlett." Bill responds: "Oh, you must want my father. My name's Bill." Many people in the company report that this is how they first realized that they were expected to call *everyone* by his or her first name.

Bill Hewlett used the sense of discomfort often felt in associating with someone of higher status and the consequent desire to act appropriately to dramatize an important learning point. The encounter is thus memorable even though it focuses on an apparently minor practice. For many at HP the story's underlying point is that they are a company of people who work together and who, despite differences in assignments, skills, and experiences, are not different in worth as individuals.

In each of these examples, executives were searching for

opportunities to put flesh on the abstractions of their philosophy and values, and they sought to do so in dramatic and meaningful ways.

Practicing What You Preach. Employees are sensitive to how serious managers are about a particular emphasis, and they often judge seriousness by how consistent others are. If the day-to-day behavior of top executives or others with influence is not consistent with their espoused vision, employees become cynical.

In a *Fortune* 500 firm, managers complained that although their president was pursuing innovation as a key theme, they could tell he did not really mean it. When Thomas Peters (1980) looked at how the president spent his time, he found that only 5 percent of this president's day was spent on things related to innovation. In contrast, when Patrick Haggerty was CEO of Texas Instruments, he stopped by the R&D labs on his way home from work every day and spent a lot of time in division reviews focusing on new products. Haggerty apparently knew the importance of letting the way he spent his time say what he valued.

The consistency between big ideas and mundane management behavior is not just a matter of managing a public image. Some of the most influential and popular stories I have heard are about the behavior of people when they are not on dress parade. For example, in one story at Hewlett-Packard, Bill Hewlett, then company president, was doing some photocopying after hours wearing a white lab coat. (An interjection by many storytellers: "Bill really loves R&D, and he often puts on a lab coat and spends time out in the labs.") A new secretary who was closing up the laboratory saw him and asked accusingly, "Were you the one who left the lights and copy machine on last night?" "Uh, well, I guess I did," was the reply. "Don't you know that we have an energy-saving program in the company and that Bill and Dave have asked us to be particularly careful about turning off lights and equipment?" she asked. "I am very sorry. It won't happen again," returned Bill.

The sequel to the story is that two days later the secretary passed Bill, who was now dressed in a suit and wearing a name tag, when she visited the main office building. "Oh no," she thought. "I chewed out the company president!"

The most important point for those who told the story was not that Bill had forgotten to follow his own energy-saving policy but that he did not pull rank on the secretary. Like everyone else, he felt bound by the rules he set, and he really seemed to believe in one of HP's ideas: "We are family here; we treat people with respect and as equals."

Through persistent attention to the details of time spent, memos written, and questions asked, managers can give credence to the key themes they espouse. Furthermore, if their offstage actions are consistent with their public performances, they add significantly to that credibility.

Creating an Administrative System That Embodies Vision

The simple creation of an organizational design and procedures does not necessarily communicate and give direction to accomplishing a particular vision. Management must make a significant effort to help people understand the reasons behind the administrative practices and structure and to show how they represent and symbolize the company's vision. After considering how to create administrative practices and procedures that can serve as symbols of organizational purpose, we will explore how the administrative structure and human resource systems in an organization can provide a context that will facilitate the development of organizational skills over the long term. This is a tall order and not something that is ever done perfectly. We will, therefore, consider as well some of the major difficulties firms encounter as they attempt to accomplish the symbolic and developmental functions when they create administrative systems.

Create Systems That Are Symbols. The major concern in considering the symbolic value of administrative systems here is whether they are consistent with the overarching values or vision the company is trying to communicate. Thomas Watson (1963), a past CEO of IBM, argued that managers should take three general steps to create a company that would be successful in the long run: (1) start by describing your beliefs, important themes (for example, "IBM means service"), and values; (2) next, operationalize those beliefs in programs, policies, organizational structure, and incentive systems consistent with the beliefs; and (3) change the operationalizations whenever necessary to remain competitive while still being consistent with the beliefs.

The important idea here is that the beliefs, not the programs, are enduring. Frequently, programs or systems come to symbolize important values and subsequently are outdated. Managers must keep in mind bedrock beliefs and never let programs become empty routines that are kept beyond their usefulness. Of course, this is easier said than done. Creating programs that are consistent with and are actually accepted as symbolic of a shared vision is not easy. Changing an established symbolic program may be even more difficult.

One company decided to communicate their value of treating people as equals by changing their pay system so that everyone, including the nonexempts, received a salary. The move from hourly pay to salary for nonexempts was primarily symbolic because of government regulations concerning payment of overtime, but management nevertheless wanted to communicate the value of equality. In spite of the good intentions, however, many employees found fault with the new system.

During the heat of the criticism, the company president took two full days to visit with employees throughout the company (largely at their work stations) to understand what had gone wrong. He found a number of problems, like the fact that employees were used to getting two paychecks a month and receiving the first one early enough to make house payments. The new "salary-for-all" system caused problems for both of these employee expectations because they received only one paycheck a month on the ninth, rather than on the first, of the month. The president personally oversaw a number of changes in the program and took responsibility for the early criticism. Within a month or two, most employees saw both his commitment and the purpose behind the new system. Four years later, when I gathered stories in this company, the story about this new pay system and its initiation was a popular and positive one.

However, cutting such symbolic programs can be very un-

popular. In this same company, human resource executives ago-
nized for some time about whether to discontinue several highly
popular programs in one division. Previous to its acquisition,
this division had established such paternalistic programs as laun-
dry facilities for employees to do their wash at work, showers
for employees who jogged at lunch time, and a chapel for private meditation. These practices proved expensive to duplicate
when the division was slated for expansion to new buildings.

These programs were cut, and as a result, a number of the
division's employees left the company. Human resource executives in the company guessed that it took almost six years of
considerable effort to reestablish a feeling of goodwill toward
the parent company in that division. They believed that they
would have saved time and considerable expense, not to mention bad feelings, if they had begun earlier to rotate some line
managers, employees, and human resources executives through
the home office, if only for a matter of months. They feel they
should have spent more time on helping people in the new division understand the parent company's philosophy before any
dramatic changes were made. Only when employees see how
the company's philosophy and values work will they be able to
understand the symbolic value of new programs. In this case,
employees in the acquired division needed some time to both
understand what was for them a new company philosophy (or
vision) and be reassured that the programs embodying it would
eventually benefit them (a faith in fairness concern). Company
executives had provided no such help, and their actions were
thus met with great resistance.

Organizational systems and practices may come to symbolize the organization's very essence and how it differs from
the outside world. But they can only do so if at least some of
the practices and systems are unique. People who dress alike but
in uncommon ways, for example, come to see themselves as potentially different from others. At Electronic Data Systems
(EDS), for example, when employees seem not to understand
the company's philosophy, people will say that they need to return to headquarters to "have their suits blued." This refers to a
fairly strict dress code in the company, but more than proper

dress is implied. The dress symbolizes a different orientation, a separateness from the ways of other organizations. This can also be seen as the underlying reason for the salary-for-all program mentioned earlier. That program was difficult to administer, but it was different and communicated a sense of that difference to all employees. Even new employees and outsiders, who cannot understand the more subtle, and perhaps more substantive, aspects of the company's character, can recognize these overt symbols. The symbols remind people to think of this place as somehow special. The symbols also function to encourage employees to learn the more subtle understandings and social conventions they represent.

Most companies miss significant opportunities to highlight the symbolic nature of their systems and practices when they fail to write a company history or to take time occasionally to memorialize the company's development and its significant achievements. Such events as beer busts to celebrate the accomplishment of division goals or birthday celebrations or company picnics can all lend credence to the belief that this company is different. However, managers should concentrate on finding ways to communicate their concern and values in appropriate and unique ways.

A recent and very successful example of how this can be done comes from Charles Feld, the vice president of management services at Frito-Lay. Feld's group had been working overtime for months to meet several critical deadlines. They were also responsible for numerous aspects of the company's move to a new headquarters. Feld did not detect any burnout or waning enthusiasm among the group during this period. However, when he dropped by the new headquarters complex on a Sunday afternoon to visit with people as they moved in, he could tell that the spouses of his employees were not as enthusiastic.

His concern has been to establish a feeling of group pride and opportunities for individual development that would encourage people to stay with the company for a long time. He has also encouraged managers not to require overtime but to involve employees in understanding and setting deadlines so they would feel responsible to keep deadline commitments and do what it takes to meet them. Further, he helped to renegotiate commitments when they turned out to be unrealistic. Feld sensed that while his plan had indeed motivated employees, their spouses had borne an unusually heavy cost during the past months. He worried that they would not feel appreciated or involved with the group's accomplishments and pride. He also realized that unhappy spouses could eventually undermine employees' enthusiasm.

Feld decided he should find a way to say thank-you to employees and especially to their spouses. He organized a gala black-tie dinner for which he commissioned the chamber orchestra of Dallas. Nothing was spared to make this evening a special occasion. He gave a brief speech expressing gratitude for employees' pride in their work and for the quality of their efforts. He also mingled and expressed his feelings to individuals.

I recently had two research associates gather cultural data in this division. People we interviewed frequently used the black-tie dinner as a way of proving that this was an unusual place to work. Their pride in their accomplishments, their loyalty to Feld, and their desire to remain and grow with the company were frequently expressed in the same breath with their recounting of the black-tie dinner. It was as though the dinner was their reason for feeling the way they did. Of course, dinners alone do not produce such positive feelings. But in this group the black-tie dinner is one of several practices or events that have come to symbolize a strong feeling of uniqueness.

The dinner was a spontaneous idea. It is not, and could not be, a regular event. It was the result of an ongoing effort to "say" something clearly by means of programs, policies, and practices. The appropriateness of the dinner to the moment, the consistency with ideas Feld was trying to teach, and the uniqueness of the event were the key elements that made for its success.

The black-tie dinner is not a system in this organization in that it is not something done regularly. However, most other managers in the division stage smaller versions of this idea with their employees. Picnics or a special celebration are frequent occurrences. In this sense, Feld has encouraged the development of a "system" of spontaneous celebration that is triggered not by the calendar but by events or accomplishments worth appreciating.

Create Systems and Practices That Develop Skills. My general observations about how systems can create a context that develops organizational skills embodying organizational purpose fall into four categories: (1) how new employees are selected, (2) how they are developed and rewarded, (3) how decisions are made about whom to retain, and (4) how to centralize initially to teach people the link among systems, practices, and character, and then decentralize to develop people's ability to govern themselves with these understandings. The first three categories are consistent with William Ouchi's (1981) suggestions in *Theory Z.* The fourth is borrowed from Phillip Selznick (1957).

1. *Selection:* Companies that develop a strong character that perseveres select people who are not only competent but also already share many of the values espoused in the company. While other organizations may tend to focus on competence alone, these companies screen people through as many as seven to ten interviews, largely with people throughout the company with whom they might some day work rather than with personnel specialists. The interviews will often aim primarily at trying to ascertain whether the candidate will "fit." Interviewers also try to describe the company's values clearly enough so the candidates can decide whether the company fits their individual values.

Potential managers, or other key contributors, may be asked to come to work as interns rather than directly out of school in another attempt to find out about fit. Universities, areas of the country, and headhunter firms are also carefully evaluated to ensure that they will provide people whose values are compatible with those of the organization seeking to perpetuate its character. Such people are more likely to cherish stories about company values because its values are close to the values they bring with them.

2. *Development and rewards:* Training in these strong-

character organizations tends to be different as well. Human resource executives in one such company, Hewlett-Packard, claim
that close to one-third of every training program a company
sponsors (including orientation, technical training, and management development) is devoted to talking about how the particular training relates to the "HP way" (the company philosophy). They explicitly make the point that skills per se are in-
adequate for success in the company. An HP employee must
understand and implement the company philosophy in order to
work well with others and to help the company be successful,
according to these executives. Employees are thus motivated to
learn the values, and they find concrete stories one of their best
means of understanding those values. As a matter of fact, human resource managers have from time to time gathered stories
that illustrate the application of the HP way for use in training
programs.

In addition, Hewlett-Packard executives formally encourage the concept of a "career maze," claiming that carefully
planned careers are rarely possible. Instead, employees should
try to help out where needed (thus wandering mazelike through
various jobs). However, over the long run, employees should
have experience in several different divisions and functions
within the company. The result is that over their career in the
company, most managers become experts in how the pieces of
the company fit together, and, though this is not the explicit intent, they become storytellers. (They are called "graybeards"
at Hewlett-Packard.) They are able to tell stories to newcomers
that help them see the big picture and give them perspective
about how the company works.

There are many graybeards at HP because of another set
of company policies and procedures. HP tries to keep people
with the company long term. You cannot have graybeards who
share experience in the company and a common stock of stories
and understandings to help new employees if turnover is high.
These companies that work at maintaining character tend to
have profit-sharing and stock-option plans available to a large
group of their employees. (At HP all employees are eligible after
one year of employment.) These companies are likely to have
generous pension plans. The resulting "golden handcuffs" en-

courage people to remain with the company and to learn and pass on the values and conventions of the company character.

Management systems can also be designed to reward people for acting in harmony with company values. In the past, HP has conducted a "personnel audit" each year in which executives review a company division to determine whether the division general manager and staff have consistently followed the HP way. They sampled twenty or thirty employees from the division and conducted in-depth interviews to make their determination. The results of these interviews were put in the division general manager's file and figured heavily in the evaluation of his or her performance. Such efforts make it more likely that employees will see the company management as seriously interested in the consistency between behavior and values.

3. *Retention:* Relative to other organizations, companies that seek to develop their character are much more likely to fire people because they have been dishonest than because they are incompetent. The reason is that it takes time to learn how to be fully consistent with the company philosophy. It is often a mistake to be strict with employees regarding their competence if they have been with the company less than five years. It makes more sense to evaluate them, at least in the short run, on whether they are honestly trying their best to learn. If they shirk or are otherwise dishonest, then they cannot be trusted in the long run. If they are somewhat incompetent at first but are willing to learn, then they can probably contribute in time.

Many organizations focus strictly on competence. However, at HP, one of John Young's self-appointed tasks when he was a senior vice president was to review all involuntary turnovers. His goal was to ensure that managers tried to work with the person and, if incompetence was the primary problem, to discover whether attempts had been made to find the person a position elsewhere in the company. However, if a person had been clearly dishonest, then there was apparently little mercy for him or her. For employees to see others getting away with selfish and dishonest actions would be to encourage distrust and to display inconsistency with the company's values. "This company is large enough that we can find a place for almost everyone we hire to be productive if they are honest and work hard,"

Young explained to me, "but we cannot tolerate someone who doesn't give his or her best or who tries to cheat the company."

The result of such programs and policies is that people in this organization have enough time to learn a somewhat abstract and often complex philosophy and the myriad social conventions that support it. However, where high turnover, inconsistent management behavior, or systems promote game playing and self-protection, people learn how to survive and even profit at the company's expense.

4. *Centralize, then decentralize:* To create administrative structures and systems that accomplish the three preceding purposes, many organizations need to first centralize their operations to encourage executives to spend significantly more time in the development of the systems. For example, at Frito-Lay, Charles Feld decided to have a group of young managers who were new to the company report directly to him rather than through a senior executive. He spent time coaching them, helping them develop new systems, structures, and practices and relate their efforts to the character of Frito-Lay. He presented them with an overall picture of the firm's strategic needs and then encouraged them to make proposals to him about how their particular groups should be structured and the activities in which their groups should engage.

When Feld received their reports, he asked them invariably how their proposed systems and priorities related to the larger vision. He called what he was doing "nesting their vision." He assumed that if he continued to require them to focus on the larger purpose of the organization and understand how their daily activities, structures, and systems fit into the larger company, then he could develop their understanding to the point that they would eventually require much less supervision. Once he felt that they were not simply following rules without insight, he gave them significantly greater freedom.

Creating Organizations That Embody Vision

This chapter started with lessons learned by Esso Chemicals executives. We have considered the actions of other executives that teach similar lessons about how to develop organizational character embodying a shared vision. We have observed that managers must be willing to dig into the details of new systems, structures, rewards, and practices. But most importantly they must be willing to change their own behavior. They must learn to use their own actions to demonstrate new priorities and to empower others to improvise and develop new execution skills and conventions.

I have thus far used examples from people at the top and in the middle of organizations to illustrate the negotiation and embodiment of vision. Most of the literature on cultural change in business focuses on the role of top management in performing these leadership functions in organizations. My experience suggests that those in the middle may, in some ways, be more able to do something about building organizational character than are those at the top. In the next chapter I specifically address what those in the middle can do with organizational character in their own areas and how they can influence the rest of the organization. I also consider what they must do to earn permission to develop character in their part of the organization.

6

Influence Corporate Character from the Middle: Not Waiting for the CEO

Perhaps the most frequent response to my efforts to teach managers about organizational culture and character is the complaint that until the CEO decides to do something, there is little others in the organization can do that will make a difference. This chapter is devoted to my counterargument to that perception. Consider the following example.

Some fifteen years ago, Charles House was assigned to be the research manager of a new ventures group in the Colorado Springs division of Hewlett-Packard. He had been given what some thought were the dregs of the organization. The group had not produced a significant innovation for years and had gradually seen its better engineers leave. Some compared it to an expansion ball club, a collection of new misfits and old has-beens. The group generally had a very negative image of themselves.

House began by trying to take inventory. He interviewed members of the group to discover the potential for significant innovation. What he found was disheartening. He learned that they were not reading any of the current top journals in their field and that they were unaware of what people in other divisions of HP were doing that related to their efforts. He also discovered that they were unaware of what competitors were doing. Indeed, few in the division even talked to each other about what they were working on.

He concluded that because few of the current projects were promising and because the engineers had little awareness of their surroundings, he would use a significant share of his first year's research budget to pay for travel, journals, and attendance at conferences. He required that every engineer spend at least one week during the first year at other locations in the company, and to spend one week visiting potential customers to learn about their needs. House also required the engineers to keep up to date in the leading journals in the field. He further insisted that some of the engineers attend conventions where competitors were selling, explaining, and demonstrating their current work. He held regular meetings at which people were assigned to report on what they had seen, read, and learned.

Excitement grew daily. Engineers began to have a feel for what was needed, what was possible, and what no one else had done. They began to feel like a team that had something important to do and could only do it right by working together. As their ideas blossomed and took form, they had the feeling that they were united in a cause, that they held within their group great secrets, and that these secrets, when acted upon, would make a real difference in the world.

During this time, House had to explain some unusual budget allocations to corporate headquarters and why his division was not spending dollars on current projects. He occasionally exaggerated the progress they were making. He also spent much of his time taking incipient ideas to people he trusted in the company for their evaluation and help in linking up with others who were doing similar work.

Within a year his group had several projects going. Two and one-half years afte his arrival, the division produced an innovation significant enough that it was awarded "Achievement of the Year" by *Electronics Magazine* and was subsequently included in the *Computer Design* "Hall of Fame." House was honored for "distinguished international contribution to the engineering and scientific community" in 1986 by the Society of Manufacturing Engineers. He just completed a five-year assignment as the director of corporate engineering for Hewlett-Packard.

House is an excellent illustration of what I call a "border guard." He was able to take a group of people and instill them with some faith in themselves. He encouraged a sense that this group had something to contribute. He protected his group from the incursions of the rest of the system while these engineers were forming and building a new vision and image of themselves. Although he was in the middle of the company, he helped his group develop a distinctive character in the division. We can see clearly all of the elements of organizational character in this division. The division spent time developing a shared vision by seeking information and continually sharing their views about competitors, new developments, opportunities, and division strengths. The group also learned to nest its vision within the company's needs and opportunities. House diffused outside intervention so he could reward engineers for early efforts and develop their faith in the fairness of the division. The shared vision and faith in fairness focused and motivated employee efforts to develop new skills.

House did not help create something that was entirely different from the rest of Hewlett-Packard. Indeed, he helped many of the people who had formerly been insulated from the parent company to have greater contact with it. Nevertheless, his actions led to a sense of pride, to distinctive division skills, and to an example for the rest of the company that was significantly different from what had existed previously at that division and in some other parts of the company.

House's example should give hope to managers who wonder whether they can do anything to affect the company in which they work. In fact, it may be easier to influence a company from House's position than from the top of an organization. Teaching, persuading, and modeling new ways of thinking and acting are often easier when a manager has face-to-face contact with all or most of the members of the group. However, we must recognize and overcome several dangers if someone within an organization wants to create a unique character for a unit within a larger organization that is not making similar changes or has already made them. Let us turn now to some of these concerns.

Earning Permission to Be Unique: Create an Exchange

I first started thinking about the idea of border guards after talking to a colleague, Kerry Patterson. He defined "border guard" as someone on the border of two cultures who influenced traffic between the two. As an example, he told of his experience as an officer in the Coast Guard in the early 1970s during the Vietnam War. He was responsible for a group of bright college graduates who had joined the Coast Guard largely to avoid the draft. Most of these men were bored and cynical about the military because their talents far exceeded the jobs they had been assigned, and they were not allowed to deviate from traditional practices. They were very capable of finishing their weekly work in the first two or three days of the week. My colleague saw no reason why they should have to stay around during the last half of the week if their work was indeed done. He thought they could rotate responsibility for manning the phones and a few other odd details.

Patterson's proposal met considerable resistance from his superiors. However, he was able to argue that it would be much easier to curb the excesses in longer hair and insubordination that had characterized this group in the past if he could achieve some kind of concession. Dubiously, his superiors said they would give him a trial period. He sat down with the group and told them that he was willing to stake his reputation and military career on their ability to demonstrate the propriety of their work-saving ideas. He helped them see what was at stake for them. He explained to them that while it seemed silly to these college graduates to keep their hair short and to behave in military fashion when in public, that was the price for having up to two days a week of extra free time. They were willing to take on the challenge.

The group became the highest performing and most highly regarded group on their base. Patterson sponsored after-work social activities and was able to build a strong esprit de corps among these young men and their families. The group members made innovative suggestions for improving their work and indeed were able to even further reduce the time it took to finish their weekly work.

Shortly following Patterson's departure, the new officer appointed to the group quickly changed everything back to the "hurry-up-and-wait" attitude that had preceded Patterson's administration. The new officer was apparently threatened by the group's self-confidence and initiative. However, his biggest challenge was to maintain the exchange relationship with the rest of the organization. A border guard must manage some tension between different cultures. It requires sticking your neck out and facilitating some compromise. The new officer felt it was not worth the hassle.

This example illustrates well the importance of developing an exchange relationship with those who evaluate the group and its efforts. A would-be border guard must avoid naively initiating changes without giving thought to why others in the organization should permit these changes. In this case, Patterson was able to exchange what was relatively peripheral to members of his group (long hair and a sullen attitude) for the opportunity to be free from hours of meaningless drudgery and simply waiting around. From the point of view of the larger organization, concerns about external image and insubordination were solved. The group also delivered an efficient, high-quality service. Exchanges must make sense to be accepted, and in this case Patterson was able to discover a way to make that exchange clear and to help others see why it fit the larger Coast Guard context. That is not to say that his group followed the military culture completely. It was clearly very different. It maintained the trappings of the external culture in terms of dress and behavior with external publics, but the group's norms, values, and assumptions were actually quite different. In this case, they simply had to be aware of the external organizational culture and conform to its most observable values.

However, this example from the military suggests that even such successful efforts as Patterson's are likely to be short lived because they are maintained only at the cost of vigilance and of keeping intact a group of people from the outside with a similar culture of their own. Yet a group within an organization cannot only create its own character but also, as a result, influence the rest of the organization. The example of Charles Feld, vice president of management services (responsible for computer systems and systems development) at Frito-Lay, may help to illustrate this point.

I observed Feld's efforts as he sought to create a sense of the special contribution his group could make. It seemed to me that he was trying to create a distinctly different subculture within the larger company. Frito-Lay was characterized by high turnover, which resulted from a very competitive promotion and reward system. A person either succeeded or was told to find employment somewhere else. When Feld was hired from IBM to become vice president, his division was experiencing 38 percent turnover per year. He discovered that the division was unable to deliver high-quality new systems to accounting, plant management, and sales groups because it could not maintain an intact task team for the time it took to develop a new system. He was also concerned that there was very little of what he called "bench strength" to help when unexpected new systems were requested.

Feld began looking for people whose skills were comparable to those of former employees but who were more interested in staying with the company for a while. These people were not strictly systems developers and were hired not from other companies but directly out of school. He was taking a risk in hiring people who would have to stretch and who were inexperienced compared to those hired previously. His hope was, however, that by challenging these young people and supporting their development, he could obtain a sense of commitment and progress and a feeling of pride among them that would encourage them to stay and grow with his organization.

By and large, Feld's strategy worked. Within four years his division had the lowest turnover in the entire company: 10 percent per year. He was faced with a problem entirely different from the one that had confronted him initially. He now had a group of people asking about career paths and what long-term opportunities they could expect in the company. He saw this problem as the result of the success of his strategy and worked willingly and creatively to address these concerns.

Seeing that Feld was indeed creating a very different culture within the larger company, I shared with him a "Doonesbury" cartoon about a translator for the U.S. ambassador to China. The ambassador begins by accusing the Chinese of human rights violations, which she translates as greetings from the president of the United States. The ambassador continues his criticisms, and she translates them as greetings from the vice president. After the speech the ambassador asks the translator why the Chinese audience was applauding him. The translator admits she took a few liberties with his text. "A few liberties? What did my speech end up being about?" "Ball bearings, sir." "I spoke for forty-five minutes on ball bearings?" "Yes, sir. And you were spellbinding!" The clear implication for me was that Feld was the counterpart of the translator in this cartoon, a border guard who had to work hard to screen out some "bad vibes" from the larger culture.

Almost without hesitating, Feld's response was, "I don't think you understand. I am a good border guard because I believe in what the top management is doing. I may not agree with the way some programs get implemented, but I believe that we are doing exactly what is best for the company. My problem is how to help those in my group understand and support what we are trying to do."

Feld illustrates the ability of a border guard not only to buffer and seal off a group of people but also to connect them to the rest of the company. However, he went beyond merely connecting people with the larger organizational needs. During his first four years as a vice president, Feld was able to convince top management that his group's contribution to the development of new systems could be a key competitive advantage for the firm. He suggested that they develop hand-held computers and supporting pricing and accounting systems that would help salespeople adjust prices on the spot in a given regional area of competition. Because he had delivered in the past and because he understood the capacities of his own group and had their support, he was able to present a vision of what the company could do and how his group could contribute significantly. What his group delivered buttressed the current strategy and helped change it to some extent and made it even more regionally based than it had been previously.

Feld's group had other influences on Frito-Lay. Whereas Feld's group had imported managers from other parts of the company before his arrival in 1982, the systems development group in 1986 exported eleven managers to work in other parts of the company. These managers had even at that early date begun to influence other parts of the company with a similar focus on understanding the overall strategy, linking what their smaller group was doing to that strategy, and encouraging the development of what Feld called a career system.

House, Patterson, and Feld represent somewhat different border guard stances. They also differ in the degree to which they could influence the larger organization. However, each border guard illustrates how people in the middle of organizations can create a distinctive subgroup character—people excited about their ability to contribute and to be treated fairly, who have distinctive skills, and who develop a vision about how they fit in the larger organization. Each border guard had to find a way to position his group in the larger organization. Each created an exchange relationship that, although different in its content and impact on strategy, showed how the group could benefit the organization and thus why it should be allowed (even encouraged) to differ.

Border guards and their groups also can take negative or antiorganizational stances. I will next present a general description of the considerable variety in border guards I have observed and a summary of the common functions they perform.

Varieties and Functions of Border Guards

Following these early experiences that sensitized me to the concept of border guards, I have observed them in many organizational settings and positions. They can inhabit almost any

level of an organization. For example, I have seen a very effective border guard who was a first-line supervisor, the lowest-
level manager in an organization, and I have also seen another
highly effective one who was the chief financial officer, the
number two executive in a company. Indeed, if we think of the
CEO as someone who represents the organization to the outside, negotiates with shareholder representatives, and seeks to
position the organization, we could say that CEOs can and
should function as border guards.

Border guards may be unofficial or official. At Hewlett-
Packard, for example, the official role of the division general
manager is to be a border guard. Divisions are seen as "feudal
baronies." The division general manager is given the task of
creating a unique subgroup with high esprit de corps that han-
dles its particular market and competitive needs in the way that
the group and the division general manager deem most appropriate. By contrast, in the Higgins Equipment Company, the
most influential person in the organization had created within
his R&D group a strong subculture that was taken into account
in every decision executives made. But this man did not have a
formal position within the organization. He literally refused to
be a manager.

Border guards also can operate with groups of varying
sizes. I have seen a border guard creating a unique and exciting
group with four other people, and I have also watched border
guards influencing and creating a sense of subgroup uniqueness
with several thousand employees.

What is consistent in the nature of border guards are the
particular functions they perform. Let us consider three key
functions involving perception, politics, and practicality.

1. *Perceptual function:* Border guards help others understand their place in the organization and find meaning in what
they do. A border guard typically helps people create a language
that they then use to interpret and talk about what is happening
in the organization. They also use this language and way of seeing the world as a means of reinterpreting the history of the
organization and of the group. Finally, in a way analogous to
the "Doonesbury" cartoon character, a border guard may help

translate messages that come from the rest of the organization so that they can be understood in the terms that the subgroup has learned to use. This process operates not only with the border guard translating for the subgroup but also the other way. That is, the border guard also helps people outside of the subgroup to view the group appropriately and to see its role in the overall organization.

2. *Political function:* In this case, the border guard acts as a buffer for the group. He or she protects the group and negotiates trades and deals, enabling the group to maintain its focus and its ability to develop a competence. This role suggests that as the group comes to have a competence, and as the rest of the organization comes to see what the group can offer, the border guard uses these perceptions to increase the power or influence of the group and helps to position the group in that regard.

3. *Practical function:* The border guard also communicates to people within the group the constraints and practical aspects of dealing with the outside world. Thus, as we saw from Patterson's example, the border guard teaches people what the outside culture will and will not accept in terms of deviance. He or she also helps the group work through its own preferences and thus make trade-offs between peripheral values and cherished values.

People who adopt very different orientations toward how to relate to the rest of the organization can perform these functions. Charles House, Kerry Patterson, and Charles Feld provide useful illustrations of different orientations. For example, House developed a competitive relationship with other groups within his company, whereas Patterson managed a counterculture that nevertheless fit within the larger organization. Feld, on the other hand, created a group that sought to influence the whole organization in a way that nested within the company's larger vision.

Imagine border guards taking different positions along a continuum of the degree of integration with a larger outside culture. Feld represents, on the one hand, an effort to integrate within the larger culture, whereas House may represent the creation of a common enemy of outsiders, including competitors of the firm, as a way of building esprit within the subgroup.

Patterson might also be on the less-integrative end of the continuum; however, his role was to buffer the subgroup and to help it fit within and be accepted by the outside group. I have noted several examples of even more countercultural subgroups within organizations. These groups are often subversive. In the Higgins Equipment Company, for example, a man named Brown saw himself and his group as the butt end of jokes and at the low end of the organization's status hierarchy. They represented the production function in an organization that highly valued research. Brown did not have a college degree, and the history of his group was that they had typically been seen as the "lower-class citizens" who did the company's routine work. Brown's response was to share stories frequently within his group about how he had sent back designs from those "know-nothing" engineers. He told the engineers that they did not know how to make plans practically, in a way that could be produced efficiently, and he continually sent their plans back for rework. In addition, Brown would come back from meetings with the vice presidents (he was the only member of the executive committee who was not a vice president) and regale his subculture listeners with tales about how he had brought up things that none of the others had thought about. These actions created a sense of the rest of the organization as common enemy for this subgroup and developed a very negative and subversive role for his group.

My point is not to argue from a normative point of view that Feld is good and Brown is bad. In reality, the Higgins Equipment Company executives that Brown worked with had fostered the negative role Brown and his subgroup played. Instead, I suggest that border guards evaluate their situation and discover how they might best create a group that would provide the meaning, the esprit de corps, and the opportunity to meet subgroup and personal needs in an organization. That may occasionally include protecting oneself from the larger organization if the larger organization is hostile and inattentive to subgroup needs.

Some Advice to Border Guards

The following specific advice for border guards is based on my observations of their functions and orientations within organizations. I do not have a systematic theory that covers every situation because, as just noted, each situation might differ to some extent. However, my advice is generally applicable across a variety of situations, and I offer it in the spirit of suggestions that might be evaluated and discarded if they do not apply in a particular situation. Most of my advice assumes that it is usually better to start by trying to set up an exchange rather than an adversarial relationship with the rest of the organization.

1. *Solve your own problems first:* Feld is an excellent example of someone who was successful in not only creating a subgroup but also influencing the larger organization because he started by solving his own problems. His group was not meeting its deadlines. It could not do so until changes were made, and Feld used his early success in solving production problems as a lever to create an exchange in the organization. Individuals and groups that are seen as not in control of their own situation are rarely allowed to create their own subgroup character, let alone influence the rest of the company.

2. *Find your own space:* After some early successes at meeting output deadlines, Feld was able to obtain some concessions from the larger organization. For example, he brought top executives into his area to show them how spread out his group was and the dilapidated nature of their working environment. He obtained $100,000 and a new building area and was able to fix up the surroundings and pull his group together into one place. The striking green carpets of the newly furnished building led people to call the area "Emerald City" and to dub Feld "the Wizard of Oz." Feld thus provided them both with a symbol of their uniqueness and unity and with a place where the group could interact and build a common language and common views. House, on the other hand, had separate facilities for engineers, but they did not use them. He created meetings

and joint learning opportunities that helped group members to interact and think of themselves as a group.

3. *Nest your vision:* Feld, Patterson, and House illustrate different ways of positioning their groups. In each case, they found a way to identify commonalities between the needs of the outside group and the abilities or interests of the subgroup. They encouraged and sold the concept of these commonalities to people within and without the group to create an image in the minds of all concerned about the group's position and importance. Each of these three spent hours listening to people in and out of their group to understand the needs of the organization and the capacities and concerns of the group. Their increased understanding helped them suggest how the group could contribute.

4. *Be clear about trade-offs and constraints:* Patterson illustrates well the importance of helping group members see the trade-offs in achieving an exchange with the organization. He helped them identify their pivotal values—what they wanted most—and helped them see what was, by contrast, more peripheral. In so doing he was able to help them fit practically into the larger context of the military.

5. *Take time to teach the group as well as outsiders:* Feld is perhaps the best example of this idea. He spent most of his time as a manager talking with individuals or small groups about how their particular project and the performance of that project related to the group's position in the organization. He spent time discussing with them the firm's strategic problems and the kind of political differences and issues involved at the top of the organization in implementing a particular strategy. He also helped users of the systems development efforts of his group understand what his group was trying to do. He helped them see the trade-offs that they faced when they asked for more quality or more rapid delivery. These actions enabled him to help people interpret or reinterpret the events within Frito-Lay. When one project group did not perform as it should have, he was able to understand and help others see this as an anomaly rather than a critical erosion in what his group could provide. In many similar ways he kept alive the idea of the group's position in the organization.

6. *Fight only if you can win and only if you have to:*
Thomas Peters and Nancy Austin (1985) have recommended
that middle managers creatively disobey orders as they attempt
to create pockets of excellence. They suggest, for example, that
someone operating in a role that is analogous to what I have
called border guards should ignore memos and paperwork requests from headquarters as a way of gaining time to produce
what the group decides is most critical. Certainly such efforts
work best when a group is performing better than any others in
the organization, which is the case for most of the examples
Peters and Austin offer. Given that position, however, it is not
critical to flaunt one's power.

As a matter of fact, a manager can often maintain the
greatest influence when he or she does not force it on others.
For example, when Feld asked for a new location, the chief
executive told the vice president of finance that two floors of
the office tower occupied by the finance group would need to
be vacated to allow the systems development group to take
over. The vice president of finance was livid. However, the chief
executive officer insisted that the systems development people
were all well-paid professionals whereas the majority of the finance people were clerk-level technicians.

Upon discovering what the CEO was doing, Feld talked
with the vice president of finance and looked for alternatives.
He discovered a somewhat dilapidated building near the tower
that had housed an insurance group previously but was largely
unused at the time. He proposed that this unwanted building
be given to him with money to fix it up. In so doing, he demonstrated his power without ever using it. He indeed could have
insisted that the finance group move. He had the power to do
so. But by keeping his sword in its sheath (Dalton and Thompson, 1986), so to speak, he demonstrated power and maintained
a relationship with the vice president of finance that has been
very helpful to him and to his group subsequently.

In a similar vein, I have observed many an idealistic border guard who fell on his or her sword. They were so sure they
were right that they felt they must fight for the ideals of their
group. But they fought a losing battle. My strong suggestion is

that it is important for someone, no matter how idealistic, to understand that it is often more important to stay alive and to fight another day. In most cases it is useful to enter an argument only when you can win. The smarter policy is to carefully husband one's influence in the organization and to avoid entering an argument only to lose it and thus demonstrate a lack of influence. Remember that the role of the border guard in most cases is to create a vision or image in the minds of outsiders and insiders of the position, momentum, and contribution of the subgroup.

7. *Cultivate allies:* In conjunction with the effort to stay alive so you can fight again another day, it is critical to recognize the importance of developing allies both within and without the group. Feld's development of a good relationship with the financial vice president was pivotal. It later aided him when he sought to sell the executive committee on the notion of spending more funds to hire additional people and to buy new equipment for his department. (This vice president in finance was a key member of the committee.) Feld also spent most of his first months as vice president working closely with a few key managers within his group to let them teach him but also to persuade them about the new directions he wanted to take. Their support was invaluable for a newcomer. In this case, he was discovering friends—people with compatible orientations—and developing a relationship with them.

However, Feld also illustrates the notion that one should be nice to "enemies" as well. He is fond of telling the stories of several in the organization whose careers have been hurt because they made friends only with those who were seen as rising stars. When some of those rising stars lost favor and left the organization or were demoted, those people who had treated the rising stars well but everyone else poorly were left high and dry. Feld's practical advice, then, is to be kind to your enemies and develop close relationships with potential friends.

8. *Create credible next steps:* House illustrates well the idea that the border guard needs to start where the group is and help it identify the next steps rather than idealistically point to what may seem to be unachievable goals (Dalton and Thomp-

son, 1986). Too many idealistic border guards I have observed paint their subgroup as the solution to every problem of the organization and fail to identify the next steps that the group needs to achieve to feel a sense of momentum. House helped his group see the need for information, obtain that information, and then pull the information together. Next he helped the engineers identify alternatives, gaps within the current information of the organization and in the scientific field they worked in, where innovation would be a contribution. In so doing, he developed a contagious feeling of winning and growing.

9. *Be consistent and dramatic, or "practice and pounce":* A border guard must practice what he or she preaches. Feld, for example, tried to sell the idea that systems developers were really salespeople, or consultants, who needed to identify clients' needs, offer a package that would meet those needs, and continually inform clients about the development, progress, and potential changes in what had been agreed upon. He was a marvelous model of doing just that. He demonstrated time and again his ability to sell ideas and to maintain a positive client relationship.

However, Feld also pounced, or looked for opportunities to jump on a situation that would dramatize his image of what the group needed to learn, as I discussed in Chapter Five. For example, he noted some paperwork needing his routine signature that proposed the promotion of an employee in his organization. However, she lacked the kind of interpersonal and client-oriented skills he wanted to foster. She was technically highly competent, but had not always maintained positive relationships with clients of the systems development group. Before his arrival at Frito-Lay, she would have been a shoe-in for promotion.

Feld refused to promote her and explained to her why. He offered her the option of moving up into a technical career path that would not involve critical client contact. She said she was sure that she had the skills necessary and wanted to prove that she did. He therefore offered her the opportunity to stay in her present position, at her present salary level, and work on a very important project that involved considerable client contact.

He suggested that by the end of this project they would both know better about her client contact skills. He then called a meeting with this young woman's supervisor and several other supervisors and discussed his decision. In so doing, he dramatized his effort to stand firm. He wanted to reinforce and value the efforts of this woman and others like her while also insisting that a particular focus, and particular skills supporting that focus, would be rewarded.

Choosing to Be a Border Guard

My intent in this chapter is to offer hope to many in an organization that they can do something with the idea of corporate character and culture. Many observers think that in most organizations the history and the ways that people have come to habitually act and see the world are so ingrained that only those with significant power and a lot of luck can do something significant to make things better. However, the notion of border guard suggests that anyone with a will and some creativity may be able to influence and develop the organizational character of at least a small group of the organization. Indeed, while one manager cannot ignore the larger organization, perhaps he or she can find a way to operate within it that brings sanity, meaning, and hope to at least part of the organization.

In conclusion, let me share an experience I had with a construction company in the South. This company was a strong competitor in the construction industry but had, along with others in this industry, fallen on hard times. The company structure gave considerable autonomy to regional operations. Each regional area had different characteristics and client needs and therefore operated differently. The company's president asked me to discuss concepts of culture with a group of managers who headed each region. Following two days of often conflict-filled discussions, we were able to isolate a number of problems in creating a strong character for the whole construction company. Most of the managers were concerned that corporate headquarters did not provide the services they wanted, and they suggested that the services did not take into account regional variations.

They complained about this or that policy and this or that mistake from headquarters.

Toward the end of our time together, I told this group about border guards. I suggested to them that a key problem was that many of them had operated as buffering border guards to the extent that they had largely cut themselves off from the larger organization. Whenever something negative happened, they blamed headquarters. I told them of the efforts of House and of Feld to bridge and build a relationship, whether distinctive or integrative, with the rest of the organization. I suggested that as far as creating a competitive character in the whole organization was concerned, they, the regional managers, were the most important group and that they could no longer continue to blame others for every problem. They had the greatest contact daily with their groups' members. They had the opportunity to find a role for their regional group, define useful policies, work out that position with corporate leaders, and develop some improvements. They could improve their understanding of the constraints the overall company faced and help reduce their groups' contempt for it. For the most part, they had failed to perform a positive border guard role well.

Following my speech, I gave the group of twenty managers thirty minutes to think through their previous two days of talk and to summarize what they were planning to do when they went home. After that period of contemplation, managers shared some of things they were going to do differently. One regional manager could hardly wait to get to his feet. He was the only New Yorker in a group of southerners and his accent stood out in bold relief. He said, "I've decided that I need to 'be a bettah bodah guahd'," and then explained how he could become a "bettah bodah guahd": He planned to spend more time helping corporate leaders see his group's unique situation and explaining to his group what headquarters was trying to do.

The concept of border guard is challenging. It does not suggest that subgroup character can be developed at will. It does, however, suggest that many people can be involved in developing organizational character, even if only in their own group. There is room for hope and for employees from all levels of the organization to contribute. They must, however, be astute. They must not miss cultural signals and political constraints. My most important message is that they must try. Almost every organization I have observed could benefit from people who were motivated to be "bettah bodah guahds."

But once a distinctive character is established, whether in the whole organization or within a part of it, it must continually be nurtured. Character stagnates and erodes when past commitments, visions, and skills are not kept alive and fresh. It also erodes when key commitments are not kept. In Chapter Seven I address how managers can avoid the erosion of organizational character.

7

Keep Faith with Corporate Character: Upholding Key Commitments

What starts out as an exciting shared vision can easily end in cynicism among employees who come to believe that "you can't trust management promises." That is just what happened in an electronics company in the Midwest.

In 1983, managers and employees at the company, a division of a major U.S. conglomerate, forged an agreement that the employees would sacrifice wage increases, make greater effort to improve productivity, and take personal responsibility for meeting commitments to customers. Management promised to provide a humanistic workplace where managers were more attentive to employee needs for development and to go to great lengths to avoid layoffs. Indeed, the promise was to consider all possible alternatives before engaging in layoffs. The commitment and agreement produced significant improvement in the organization. People took great pride in their work and considered the plant a much better place to work. The creative joint efforts of employees and management resulted in cutting costs by 30 percent. Quality also improved significantly.

After three years, however, the plant faced a significant and unpredicted drop in orders. Some of the managers were new and were not a part of the original commitment. Following significant pressure from the corporate office, division management almost immediately initiated layoff procedures. Employees were not given the opportunity to consider what they could do to address problems while avoiding a layoff. But, contrary to the earlier agreement, the first official word from management concerned the loss of jobs.

The result has been devastating. Employees have learned that the commitment to consider alternatives to layoffs was meaningless. Their faith in that commitment had previously been a major reason they were willing to make significant sacrifices. Now they do not know what to put their confidence in. Employees who remain have shown less creativity in reducing costs, improving quality, and taking responsibility to understand the company's competitive priorities. In other words, the company lost not only employees in the layoff but also, in large measure, its character.

Faith in an organization's fairness can erode quickly as shared visions and collective skills are challenged by the reality of business pressures. But unless this faith remains alive, the culture that typically results is an adversarial one where people are concerned with protecting themselves and not about working for the common good.

Additionally, whether the deviation from past commitment comes because of business pressures or because of tantalizing acquisition opportunities, shared vision and collective skills can be eroded along with faith in fairness.

Sustain Character by Keeping Critical Commitments

Executives must develop the ability to determine when a new opportunity or proposed change threatens the organization's distinctive competence. Phillip Selznick, a pioneer in thinking about distinctive competence, writes:

> The integrity of an enterprise goes beyond efficiency, beyond organization forms and procedures, even beyond group cohesion. Integrity combines organization and policy. It is the unity that emerges when a particular orientation becomes so firmly a part of group life that it colors and directs a wide

variety of attitudes, decisions, and forms of organization and does so at many levels of experiences. The building of integrity is part of what we have called the "institutional embodiment of purpose," and its protection is a major function of leadership.

The protection of integrity is more than aesthetic or expressive exercise, more than an attempt to preserve a comforting, familiar environment. It is a practical concern of the first importance because the defense of integrity is also defense of an organization's "distinctive competence." As institutionalization progresses, the enterprise takes on a special character and this means that it becomes peculiarly competent to do a particular kind of work [Selznick, 1957, pp. 138-139].

Selznick makes the distinction between critical and routine decisions. Critical decisions involve the basic character of the organization, with its distinctive competence. Certainly the time when a group is creating a new way of doing business and protecting itself from outside threats is fraught with opportunities to make important choices that will have long-lasting impact. However, when the basic direction has been decided, leaders in the firm must constantly be vigilant about the kinds of commitments the firm makes. They must be willing to make some irreversible commitments in a few areas and keep them over a relatively long period to allow for the time and focus necessary to develop a distinctive competence. Such commitments must be made with great care.

Selznick compares an organization's competence to the character or personality of an individual. He suggests that this character is formed historically as an individual makes significant commitments and thereafter keeps them. While some people make these commitments unconsciously, the existence of character is perceived by outsiders as well as by the individual when that individual follows consistently a pattern of behavior. This consistent pattern allows predictability. It enables others to form relationships with this person and trust him or her. Keeping significant commitments also allows the person to know who he or she is.

In his play *A Man for All Seasons,* Robert Bolt (1960, p. 81) portrays the feelings of Sir Thomas Moore about the importance of our commitments in giving meaning and identity to our lives. When Moore's daughter, Meg, asks him to say he approves of the activities of the King of England, although he believes the opposite, he replies: "When a man takes an oath, Meg, he's holding his own self in his own hands. Like water." (He cups his hands.) "And if he opens his fingers then—he needn't hope to find himself again."

Every organization strives to avoid the rigidity and risk that come from long-term commitments. However, if a firm is to develop a character, such commitments are crucial. Only when such commitments are honored over time will employees see the focus clearly enough and have enough time to develop a collective competence. Certainly executives must choose carefully. But they must not shirk their responsibility to make certain irreversible commitments that will give shape and form to organizational character. The essence of the character that is being created is in people's minds. It does not exist independent of their beliefs. They are, from time to time, likely to begin to doubt, or to stray from, these initial principles or commitments. Hence, their beliefs and attention must continually be pointed toward something that is stable and that continues to reenact and reprove itself to them daily. Consider the following example from David Packard at Hewlett-Packard in the early 1970s.

Executives at HP wanted to balance the firm's relatively high-risk research effort with a conservative financial policy. This balance was a key element in the company's distinctive competence. Sometimes a new product did not generate as much profit as anticipated, so executives wanted to have more than enough cash on hand and to avoid servicing interest on long-term debt that would make them focus on consistent cash flows rather than long-term innovation. Therefore, they had decided to avoid long-term debt.

While Packard, the president, was on a three-year leave of

absence to work with the federal government, some people had begun to drift toward a priority for rapid growth. When Packard returned, he found that the company was getting ready to borrow $100 million in long-term debt to cover a cash shortage that had resulted from rapid growth. Shocked at this violation of HP philosophy, the president stayed in his office for two days and examined HP's accounting records. He then called an emergency meeting of the company's top two hundred managers and made a dramatic speech: "Many have said we need to take on long-term debt. I don't believe it. Look at these figures. They tell me that our inventories and receivables have grown faster than our sales. No wonder we are cash short! We don't need long-term debt. We need *management!* And if you can't manage your inventories and receivables better than this, heads will roll! Now if we can pull together, we can work our way out of this problem within a couple of years without incurring any new long-term debt. Let's get to work!"

Within six months, the company had made up the shortage and posted a $40 million cash surplus.

In this case, David Packard was defending the integrity of the institution at a critical moment. He stated clearly what was acceptable and what was not. He acted dramatically to illustrate that the concept of avoiding long-term debt and how it related to the rest of the business was still alive. The response of HP managers, which in this case was very favorable, also added to the lesson. It suggested that they could indeed be better managers and could still have enough cash to perhaps grow more rapidly than they had in the past. They just needed to remember their basic values and skills.

The importance of keeping some long-term commitments is an abstract idea to capture. However, it is a critical one. If everything is up for grabs and if nothing is sacred, then there can be no meaning; there can be no character; there can be no long-term competence in an organization.

Perhaps we can benefit from making explicit the rough theory I used to generate advice in Chapter Five. When I suggested that managers have their best opportunity to dramatize their beliefs during crisis and that they must then show that these ideas are real by acting consistently (practicing what they preach), I assumed a model similar to that depicted in Figure 3. The model implies that people do not pay much attention to whether their expectations are being met unless they are not being met. We pay attention when our expectations are violated. We then wonder whether fundamental change has occurred and how we need to update our expectations. Most stories I hear people tell in organizations are about these crisis times. The second largest category of stories comes from times when managers have acted consistently in uncommon ways (for example, more autocratic or more considerate than expected).

Figure 3. Confirming or Disconfirming Expectations.

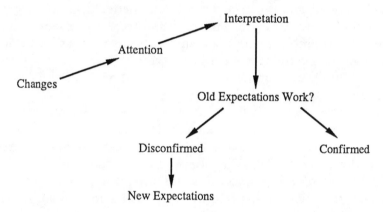

The implication for managers is that while they cannot often control the changes in the outside world that might trigger attention, they need to be aware of these moments when people are beginning to question old expectations. Of course, leaders do not have to wait for a significant crisis to happen. Sometimes the components of character get out of alignment through subtle changes that can add up to significant erosion. Packard's dramatic action at a time when drift from some basic commitments was occurring is a wonderful example of a leader declaring a crisis to draw attention to what he considered to be critical components of organizational character that were getting out of alignment.

The problem for leaders, then, is to be aware of the implications of changes for the character of their organizations, whether those changes are dramatic or gradual. Do they understand when character is at risk? Do managers see the opportunities and take them to reinforce basic commitments and expectations? Or do they fail to recognize these moments when the fiber of character may be strengthened or seriously weakened? The difference between great organizations and those that are mediocre is determined in these moments of truth.

In Chapter Two, we considered how managers could assess organizational character. As we saw from the case of Precision Instruments, character may erode in subtle ways. Managers must constantly watch for signs of loss of faith, vision, and collective skill. Much of the information that managers get about such erosion will have to come from staying in touch, from listening and observing carefully, and from introspection about what is occurring in the organization. The suggestions offered in Chapter Two about character assessment must therefore be applied in an ongoing way in the organization.

Let us now consider each of the components of character to understand how they may be eroded and what management might do to maintain a distinctive organizational character.

Avoiding the Loss of Faith

Recall that the faith motivating organizational character includes four components: faith in (1) the fairness of leaders, (2) the fairness of others, (3) the ability of the organization, and (4) one's personal ability to contribute something of value. Each of these types of faith may erode without proper nourishing.

Faith in the Fairness of Leaders. Above all, leaders must allay potential fears that they will act in their own interest rather than for the good of the whole. David McClelland (1975), who has done extensive research on power in organizations, suggests that the highest form of power is "institutional power." Such power comes from the trust of organizational members that leaders have the good of the whole company in mind and will act honorably and without favoritism to achieve that good. When we trust our leaders to act for the good of all, we give them significant power to influence us. However, they must continue to show that they are worthy of that trust. For example, when President Reagan appeared to have acted willfully and contrary to the laws of Congress, his influence shriveled.

Leaders do not have to be perfect in this regard, and organizational participants need not always agree with leaders for faith in their integrity to continue. I have listened to employees in many companies say that while they did not agree with everything management did, they were convinced that management had the best interest of the company and its employees at heart. They were convinced that if they were really concerned, they could find a hearing for their complaints. Their belief was that even though some things seemed unfair temporarily, eventually the scales would be balanced and justice would be done. Because of this trust, they were willing to give management some space to maneuver in the short term.

Leaders can show their integrity with respect to matters of fairness in myriad ways, but I have selected three critical areas of concern: (1) helping different groups within the organization to feel valued and represented, (2) handling dishonest behavior, and (3) dealing with evaluation and promotion decisions. Each of these areas has the potential to create serious concerns about the integrity and fairness of leaders if they are not handled appropriately.

In a classic study of organizational design, Paul Lawrence and Jay Lorsch (1967) discovered that organizations always face the paradox of encouraging various groups to be both different enough to manage a variety of tasks and integrated enough to obtain coordination among the different groups and achieve the overarching purposes of the firm. Indeed, the most successful organizations they observed had groups that were both more distinct in orientation and skill and more able to integrate these differences than were the less successful firms. This critical paradox must be addressed to maintain an organization's distinctive character.

Of course, groups that feel different can also feel less important. When a group feels powerless and unappreciated, its members are likely to turn to complaining or to countercultural orientations and activities. Take, for example, the man named Brown at the Higgins Equipment Company mentioned in Chapter Six. Because he felt unappreciated, he bragged about how often he had to send designs back to engineering because the engineers "weren't smart enough to do it right." His pickiness about designs was a major bottleneck for the organization.

Rosabeth Kanter (1977) offers numerous examples of autocratic, unreasonable, and emotional behavior of people in several organizations; she traces this behavior to the perceived powerlessness of their positions. She argues that management can best respond to such problems by helping these people see opportunities to influence decisions and by giving them recognition for their contributions.

However, management at the Higgins Equipment Company blamed the problem on the personality of the man rather than trying to understand and improve the situation of the head of production. For example, allowing the head of production to come to critical decision-making meetings, as well as recognizing and heralding the accomplishments of his group, would have done wonders for the self-esteem of the whole group.

Dealing with dishonest behavior and the evaluation of performance is critical if management is to maintain faith in the organization's integrity. Managers cannot afford to have people in the organization believe that they are aware of unethical behavior or very poor (or exceptionally good) performance that they fail to address appropriately. For example, middle managers in the company just mentioned were very cynical about the lack of justice in their company. These employees expended a significant amount of their emotional and creative effort in telling about top management gaffes and injustices.

However, although both dishonest behavior and employee performance must be dealt with appropriately, I believe that different principles apply to handling problems in these two areas. I offered the example of Hewlett-Packard in Chapter Six. The tendency at HP is to be relatively merciless and swift in dealing with dishonesty but quite slow and patient when it comes to dealing with poor performance (unless the poor performance is clearly dishonest shirking, not lack of ability). The HP philosophy is that punishing dishonesty is critical to maintain trust. However, employees need to have the chance to learn and develop performance skills, which involves making mistakes. Therefore, particularly with new people, the tendency is to be lenient.

Managers need to make sure that they have good data about dishonesty or performance before they act in any case. In one company, a new division general manager heard rumors about possible cheating of salespeople in the way they took credit for sales of certain machines. (They took credit for many machines that were not yet installed, which was clearly forbidden.) He looked at the data and had others help gather information. After six months, he was convinced that the rumors were true. In his company, it takes several years for people to be fired. Because he knew how much the rumors about dishonesty of a few affected the morale of other salespeople, he decided quicker action was needed. He therefore informally told the individuals that he was planning to begin the formal process to have them fired. He told them generally how much information he had and that there was no doubt that they would experience real embarrassment in the process and have great difficulty finding employment elsewhere. He said he would give them a little time to decide whether they would stay and go through the process or find employment elsewhere. Within a week these three individuals had left the company. This manager and several others in the division attribute the subsequent dramatic improvement in sales (taking this division to the top of the company) to the surge in confidence of the salespeople. The division general manager did more than reinforce honesty. However, without confidence that the system of measurement was fair and focused on appropriate things, salespeople were unwilling to give their all.

On the other hand, I argue that managers should usually be much more patient in dealing with performance problems. One reason for this patience is to make sure that action to punish or reward performance is not taken so hastily that others in the organization do not understand the reasons for such action. Managers often feel pressure from the economic realities they face to move quickly. And these economic pressures are so much more observable (through business performance measures) than erosion in employees' faith and feelings that these less obvious character components can be easily overlooked. However, to the extent that management is patient initially in informing people and giving them perspective, people come to trust that their own views have been heard. They may then allow greater freedom to managers to move quickly in times of crisis without constantly consulting with their constituencies.

An example of this kind of caution comes from a paper-making company that for fifty years was the elite company in the industry. Over the years, a number of Harvard Business School professors observed specific management actions within this firm. In one such interaction, a professor asked a plant manager why he did not consider immediately letting a man named LaPointe go, or moving him into a different role. LaPointe had been a foreman, but was obviously unable to keep up with the increased speed of the new machines, and it had become something that other foremen had begun to talk about and think was unfair. The plant manager responded: "I know that he ought to be moved, and I think Nichols [the production manager] knows it. Some of the other foremen don't know it yet. They will find out in a while and then we will be able to move him" (Dalton and Lawrence, 1971, p. 270). The plant manager was working informally to help the foremen become more aware of the difference between LaPointe's crew and other crews and to understand that this difference was largely a result of LaPointe's leadership difficulties.

When I have had students read this case, they are often critical of the plant manager. They think he was just stalling. However, time and again throughout the history of this paper company, managers were able to move very quickly because they had the essential trust and goodwill of their employees. It is just such a patient working behind the scenes to deal with the minor recalcitrance and lack of awareness of various employees that delivers such long-term flexibility. It is one thing to be fair; it is another to have people feel that you are fair.

Faith in the Integrity of Others. Somehow employees must believe not only that management is fair but also that others in the organization are trying, particularly when management is not looking, to be consistent with the organization's character. Certainly managers do not have complete control over such things, but they can help to create a climate where beliefs about fairness are more likely to occur. Managers can make some difference by (1) helping people from different groups in the organization to use the shared vision of the organization to work through their differences, (2) using the shared vision to label certain behaviors as deviant, (3) encouraging people to stop rumors about other groups and to take up their concerns personally with others, and (4) working to reduce contempt or misunderstandings between different groups in the organization to diminish irresponsible stereotyping and blaming others, which creates the impression of lack of fairness.

Managers can do much to help employees understand and use overall organizational purpose to resolve differences. For example, in one case with which I am familiar, a Peace Corps group in Africa was involved in a heated conflict. The director of the group became aware of the conflict and called a meeting to discuss it. The women in the group had asked for an increase in their allowance so they could buy some extra clothing that would allow them to dress up once a month and visit a nearby large city. The men felt that would be unfair, but the women were claiming that they had greater need. The men argued that they should also get a clothes allowance.

Rather than enter into what he thought was a relatively petty and unproductive argument that could not be resolved as it was then framed, the director asked the group to respond to some questions. He first asked, "Why did you join the Peace Corps and come to Africa?" The response from several was that they wanted to avoid the "ugly American" impressions that others had of Americans and wanted to associate with people at their own level. The director then asked, "And how are we to go about accomplishing that?" They then recited for him their understanding of their role and mission, which was to live and operate within the local context. They were to use modern technology and insights from science but apply them using the terms and needs of the people. The director then asked, "And what does that suggest about having extra money to buy American finery and to go to town once a month?" Essentially, this ended the argument. Their return to purpose and mission gave them a way to resolve their debate.

William Ouchi and I (Wilkins and Ouchi, 1983) saw similar consequences of encouraging the internalization of broad principles and purposes in a business context. During our research in one company, we saw how such sharing helps to resolve conflicts, even when they seem to be encouraged by formal incentives and rules. A personnel executive in a company that had developed a strong character told us of an experience he had while working in the Far East. One day he and the manager of the company's Far East operations had to make an emergency decision about whether to accept an unexpected opportunity for new contracts and significantly increase employment levels in one of the region's plants. They were unable to contact headquarters in the United States, and the formal company policy contained no answers. Indeed, these two managers reported to different people in the United States; one felt he would be rewarded by keeping the employment levels stable (the new contracts were short term), while the other was rewarded for adding new business. They sat down and asked themselves: "What would George do?" (George is the fictitious name of the company president some four or five levels above them in the company hierarchy.) Neither knew George personally, but they had heard him speak about the firm's general purposes and had heard their immediate managers talk about how these general ideas related to their Far East operations. They were able to decide quickly to turn down the opportunity because it did not meet some of the characteristics of the type of business and employees that fit the firm. They later discovered that top management was in complete agreement with their decision.

At least three important results come from encouraging groups, or their representatives, to use the shared vision to work through their differences: (1) differences are usually resolved in ways that benefit the whole company, (2) people in the various groups feel that decisions are made based on what is good for the whole rather than on favoritism or whim, and (3) the vision is reinforced and becomes a critical guiding force in the organization.

Managers can also help employees develop faith in others' integrity by using shared vision to teach what behaviors are inappropriate. If they will label the behaviors that are forbidden and respond consistently when they see these behaviors, then they can encourage employees to do the same. Employees will see that inappropriate behaviors are dealt with (by managers or through their own actions), and their faith in the integrity of the organization will increase.

But it is not easy to get people in social groups to confront one another openly about their concerns. Joan Emerson (1970) discusses this problem in an interesting article entitled "Nothing Unusual Is Happening." She describes research about situations in which nurses and other staff tended to minimize and make seem normal what most of us would consider inappropriate behavior by male doctors with their women patients.

Of course, what passes as normal and acceptable depends on how we label the behavior. For example, Emerson describes the frustration of two young men in Stockton, California, who tried to rob a group of thirty-six prominent women at a party where jokes and pranks filled the evening. Thus, when the would-be thieves, masked and brandishing guns, entered the room and asked people to hand over their money and valuables, everyone laughed. When the thieves shouted that they really were thieves and would shoot people who did not cooperate, the women just laughed harder. One of them playfully shoved one of the thieves. He shoved her back. As the ringing laughter continued, the men looked at each other, shrugged, and left.

What we see as deviant depends on the social context, on who we think we are, and what we think we are doing. People who are frequently reminded of "who they are" and what their purpose is are much more likely to develop shared ideas about what behaviors are inappropriate. Managers can help by being clear about a few forbidden behaviors and about why these behaviors are inappropriate given the shared vision. Managers must also be consistent about their response to violation of these rules.

In this regard, Douglas McGregor (Dyer and Dyer, 1982) uses the "hot stove rule" to describe the conditions that produce positive discipline (when employees least resent discipline). McGregor compares effective management discipline to what happens when we touch a hot stove. When you touch the stove, you know you have done something wrong; the consequence is immediate, impersonal, and consistent. A hot stove will not burn you sometimes and leave you unburned at other times. Of course, too many rules that carry consequences like a hot stove could certainly make for a rigid organization. But being clear about a few definitely unacceptable behaviors, the violation of which carries immediate, impersonal, and consistent reaction from management, can lead to clarity about what is deviant and what is not. This sounds like a prescription for how to increase employee feelings of fairness about leaders when we are discussing how to increase faith in the integrity of others. However, my experience suggests that when managers become clear and consistent about inappropriate behavior, other employees are often more willing to keep one another honest about those same behaviors.

But once employees begin to share labels of what is deviant, they need to fight the tendency to spread rumors by talking about the perceived lack of fairness of others behind their backs. Organizations where people feel good about the integrity of others are places where people generally take up their concerns with others personally and openly work through them in private.

I watched a very effective division general manager deal with some complaints she had heard about recent promotions that some people in other departments felt were unfair. She had heard rumors that several managers from other parts of her division were particularly concerned about the equity of one promotion by another manager at their level in the division. One or two managers had come to her privately to express concerns. I do not know what she said to them in those settings, but I did watch her raise the concern in a meeting of the managers at that level. She courageously said that she wanted to discuss what some might consider a sensitive issue. She first suggested that if people were not satisfied with something they saw going on, then they should go directly to the person concerned and talk about it. Spreading rumors greatly exaggerated the problem—and gave others the impression that nothing could be done. She encouraged all of them to push the issue with their peers, and even with her if they needed to, until they understood better or were able to make needed changes. "This is *our* division, not just mine," she said. "We are all responsible to make it the kind of division we feel good about."

Finally, we must realize that some of the feelings of distrust and jealousy about other groups in the organization result from lack of accurate information about the other groups. The tendency is to inappropriately stereotype and blame other groups for problems as a way of absolving our own group and building our own solidarity. This tendency can be curbed by encouraging people to address their concerns with each other in person. However, managers can also overcome the tendency to stereotype by increasing the interaction between groups and the positive information they have about one another.

One company president said that a critical role he plays in his company is to "reduce contempt." He tries to help groups understand one another by sharing information about others and by encouraging people from different groups to interact with one another. When the company passes milestones, he sponsors informal parties to which all are invited. He has provided common informal break areas and reading rooms where people from various groups will have occasion to run into one another. He has also taken a page from Lawrence and Lorsch (1967). He continues to preach the idea that groups are supposed to have different orientations and contributions. They are not doing their job if everyone approaches things precisely the same way. He encourages the differences to be openly expressed and worked through to include insights from all concerned.

An extensive literature on organizational conflict and conflict management is relevant in this regard—see, for example, Walton (1987), Alderfer and Cooper (1978), Turner and Weed

(1983), and Berg and Mirvis (1977). My point is that management must both encourage appropriate differences among groups and help them overcome their damaging suspicions and stereotyping of others if they want to maintain a special organizational character that includes all of these groups.

Faith in the Ability of the Organization. The best way to encourage faith in the ability of the organization is continued successful performance, and I will have more to say about organizational ability in the section about avoiding the erosion of organizational skill. Even skillful management cannot cover up large deficiencies in the organization's basic skills.

However, in addition to working directly with employees on developing and perpetuating skill, managers can do several things to encourage faith in organizational ability. For example, managers tend to have access to more of the organization than do other employees. Managers need to be cheerleaders and good-news carriers who share successes from other parts of the organization. Otherwise, enthusiasm wanes and hopes die in the time it takes for normal channels to deliver news. Managers who "work the halls" to uncover small successes and incremental progress and to share these momentum builders with others do much to build faith in the organization's ability.

Managers can also help by the way they respond to mistakes and failures. Rod Rougelot, the chief operating officer of Evans and Sutherland, a very successful high-tech computer graphics company, once told me that even though many of the company's designs and even some of their products had not succeeded, they had never had any "failures." "We learned from every mistake," he told me with an intense expression. As I learned more about the company, I came to understand his statement more fully. Company employees have learned to make mistakes "gracefully" (without undue fear) and to learn from them. Mistakes and poor product performance were treated as opportunities to discover what the problems had to teach rather than as chances to blame, berate, or moan. The result has been a continuing stream of high-quality and innovative products.

Of course, if managers do nothing when employees begin

to see problems with company skills, then employee faith can erode rapidly. Managers must be able to engage in repair strategies that help people understand what the problems are and what they can begin to do about them. Whether the concerns are about fairness of others or company capability, managers must find ways to encourage employees to overcome the temptation to believe that "nothing unusual is happening." Employees should be encouraged to approach each other to understand problems and work to improve their efforts. When employees take responsibility for continual improvement in the organization, they are much more likely to have faith in company abilities.

For example, Kim Fisher, an internal organizational development consultant at Tektronix, a producer of electronic measurement instruments, introduced me to several groups at the company that he calls "high-performance work systems." The employees in these groups have, over the past two to five years, developed an intense interest in the performance of their group and other groups with whom they deal. Each group is given responsibility to interact with vendors, with other groups in the company that supply parts, with engineering, with marketing and sales, and even with customers to understand the components and consequences of their task. They have learned to measure their work and make corrections to improve it. I have never seen such pride and excitement about doing quality work and continuing to improve it. In this case, faith in the ability of the organization was increased by teaching employees the components of the organizational skill and enabling them to continually improve their execution of the skill.

Faith in Personal Ability. How managers deal with mistakes and poor performance has much to do with the development and maintenance of distinctive organizational character in which people have enough confidence in themselves to give their best and continue to get better. One of the most important consequences of the approach that Rod Rougelot at Evans and Sutherland takes to mistakes is that people are given the opportunity to improve. Consequently, they are less likely to feel defeated by their mistakes. They have the opportunity to learn from their mistakes and still have confidence in their ability.

When Fred Hanson left Hewlett-Packard to take over an ailing division at Tektronix, for example, he found even more problems than he had expected. He discovered high levels of inventory in manufacturing, an engineering group that was not in touch with the customer, marketing treated as a necessary evil (to "keep the customer in line"), and centrally driven financial systems that restricted their ability to respond to their specific business challenges. However, rather than blame the employees, Hanson told them that he did not wonder that they had so many problems: only 25 of the 1,000 employees had any idea how much trouble the division was having. His solution was to teach everyone how the business works. He reduced the complexity of the numbers only a few managers had used (they had measured 30,000 labor transactions per month, for example, and he and his new controller reduced that to 30 per month) and then taught employees how to use the numbers to understand the business. He asked them to come up with ways to improve the efficiency and quality of products once they understood how to measure results. Within one year the division was profitable. Two years later it was one of the top divisions in the company, and it continues to do well. Hanson has been promoted several times since then and is currently a vice president responsible for approximately one-third of the company's business.

When people are given information, opportunity to learn, and trust to make changes, unusual results become possible. Much of the improvement comes from the feeling of self-confidence people gain when they see how their efforts contribute to making a difference. Of course, management needs to be careful that people have appropriate training and that they are not in over their heads. Otherwise, the experience of consistent failure stemming from insufficient ability can significantly damage employee self-confidence.

Avoiding the Loss of Vision

As I suggested in Chapter Two, the true test of a shared vision is not what we announce to the public but how we behave. From that point of view, managers must overcome two general problems before people can see, reinforced over time, a credible shared vision for the organization: (1) management decisions may be *inconsistent*, emphasizing first one set of priorities and then another, or (2) management may act consistently but follow such a *complex* set of priorities that others cannot see the reasoning behind the actions. Both of these problems require that management and others be continually concerned about reclarifying, simplifying, and applying consistently a particular vision. Let us consider several management practices that may help to encourage continued clarity and reclarification of organizational purposes.

Vision loses its focus when people see that the rhetoric about values like concern for employees or for high quality is thrown to the winds in the face of real economic pressures to get the product out the door. Conversely, when organizational leaders take meaningful stands that demonstrate the organization's long-term purpose and priorities in the face of short-term economic pressures, the credibility of these precarious ideas increases and is reinforced. That is, values are demonstrated by sacrifice, by doing what is hard to do, not by doing what anyone else could or would do in a given situation. That is why the example of David Packard insisting that Hewlett-Packard avoid long-term debt, cited earlier, is so powerful in the lore of the company. His was not a public-relations effort to portray the "right" image. These actions were difficult and costly in terms of short-run growth of the company. However, they showed that even in times of crisis, management was determined to follow a particular path. Such "statements" through the actions of executives "say" much more than words can ever convey.

Perhaps there are few opportunities to make such dramatic statements in the history of a company. But managers must be alert to the need to stand up and be counted when a choice has to be made between conflicting values.

Beyond dramatic statements, which are likely to be rare, managers need to demand that the organization consider carefully the addition of new products, new employees, and new programs and structures. Each addition of these and other organizational elements has the potential to take the organization along different paths or on too many paths. And beyond a concern for what is being added, managers must consider what is being continued. Do current programs and organizational arrangements continue to embody the critical purposes of the organization?

Requiring everyone to continually "nest his or her vision" for new practices or continuation of the old, then, can produce increased understanding of what is worth doing and what is not. I have watched several excellent managers habitually ask, "Why does it make sense for us to do this now?" Or they ask, "How does this [new program, proposed change] help us to accomplish our purpose?" They require everyone who makes proposals to talk about purpose and to be clear and convincing about his or her understanding of that purpose in order to function in the organization.

Of course, the world does not stay the same for long, so purposes must evolve and adapt as well. The new president of Motorola explains that top managers in his company are unwilling to be precise about the future because of the significant potential for the future to look quite different in one or two years than it does now. However, they are very interested in continuing to update their understanding of the competitive, regulatory, and technological changes they face. These managers meet every twelve to eighteen months for three or four days away from their offices to engage in what they call "strategic renewal." One of the major benefits of this process, if it is supported by continual questions about ongoing internal operations, is the increased sharing among managers throughout the company of the evolution of purpose and the ways the organization must adapt to help achieve the purpose.

I closely followed the activities of one division general manager—I will call him Tony Bertolli—as he eagerly tried to imbue his organization with a sense of purpose and excitement about achieving it. Bertolli found that he had to spend a lot of time with a particular group that represented about one-third of the division. They needed significant additions to equipment and plant and personnel, and he did not have a manager at the time who could help them link what they were doing to the changing needs of the company. After six months of intensive work with this group, Bertolli felt very good about several changes, including a transition from his leadership to the leadership of a newly hired director.

However, as he turned his attention to the whole division, he discovered that many in the other two-thirds of the division were unaware of the sometimes subtle changes in the priorities of the firm. They were therefore disgruntled when Bertolli asked for increased speed in developing some products. As he tried to persuade them, he realized that while he had been able to keep up with the political and economic changes of the firm, many managers in his division had been isolated from the changes. He simply had not taken the time to chat informally or to hold meetings to consider the implications for them of changing priorities.

Bertolli also discovered that he could not merely announce these new priorities. They had changed gradually and were subtle. He did not even have concrete evidence for everything he felt intuitively about the new priorities. His intuitions had grown and become more complex with each new piece of information. However, he was unwilling to change his style of working with his managers from understanding and commitment as the motivation for their work to command from and obedience to him as the motivation. It took Bertolli weeks of significant discussions, in groups and with individuals, to help restore understanding and confidence in the purposes and values of the division and the company. Even several months later, a few of the managers still thought that the changes he sensed intuitively were just his whims. Because they felt that their definition of the quality of the product they wanted to produce had suffered because of Bertolli's intuitions, they found it convenient to blame him rather than real changes in the company and its competitive situation.

The point I want to make with this example is that it is easy to take your eye off the ball. And even if some top managers continue to focus on the ball and are able to see the curves and sliders, unless they are continually communicating what they see, others will not understand or be able to respond quickly enough to hit the ball when it crosses the plate. Managers must engage in enough informal and formal exchanges about the organization's environment that the subtleties, as well as the dramatic changes, are registered and seen in terms of their implications for the organization. From this point of view, unless the organization lives in a rather static world, managers cannot just hold a meeting every six months to consider competitive changes if they want to encourage a vibrant understanding of organizational purpose. Ongoing talk about the environment and the implications of changes for needed organizational change must become part of the daily round or the vision will lose focus. People will see the vision as too complex or followed too inconsistently to find much meaning in it. That is a sure way to lose character.

Avoiding the Loss of Skill

Many of the problems of maintaining organizational skill stem from its tacitness. Few, if any, participants understand all that a collective skill entails. Much of the skill, as I described it in Chapter Two, is in the fingers of individuals; that is, the skill becomes intuitive, habitual, and, therefore, efficient following extended practice. The skill becomes collective through the interactions and relationships of individuals. It is perpetuated if new people develop the right habits and contacts and perspectives.

Managers do not produce the skill so much as they facilitate its development and perpetuation. The skill begins to erode when they lose touch or intuitive feel for what is in the fingertips of their people, for what it takes to accomplish certain tasks. It also erodes if relationships between key people become strained or if structural or geographical isolation makes contact between key people difficult. In addition, collective skill may be lost if new people are not stretched or brought into contact with the right people.

Keeping in Touch with Tacit Skills. One way that managers can keep themselves honest about attending to tacit skills is to pay attention to the composition of their management team. That is, if critical components of the collective skill are represented in the company's top management team or in several key managers of a division, for example, then the team as a whole is less likely to take for granted the importance of those elements. If as they consider changes and opportunities for the organization, they will give credence to the intuitions of each of these representatives concerning how critical skills will be affected, then they are more likely to preserve what is valuable.

Some have suggested that our lack of competitiveness with the foreign companies is in part related to the composition and orientations of our top management groups. For example, Robert Hayes and William Abernathy (1980) criticize managers in American organizations for their tendency to be out of touch with the real needs and opportunities in their businesses. They offer data to show that U.S. businesses spend a lower percentage of the GNP on new plant and equipment and on R&D than do those in Japan and Germany and that we are therefore not improving productivity as fast as these competitors. They claim that our inability to compete with companies from these other countries stems in large measure from a short-term and risk-averse orientation supported by top management groups, which are largely composed of financial and legal experts without operational experience in their organization's business. How can they decide what long-term risks are worth taking? How can they make judgment calls when they do not have well-developed intuitions?

In one multinational organization, for example, top management decided to build some new plants that turned out, in many cases, to have significant problems. They realized that none of their team had direct experience with overseas production and that when it came to judging location, the number of products per plant, and the relationships between plants and marketing, they had simply relied on recommendations by staff "experts" who did not have an operational feel either. These managers determined that since their future required continued emphasis on overseas production, they would (1) give two of the top twenty-five managers an eighteen-month assignment in overseas production and (2) consciously choose some new vice presidents who had the appropriate overseas experience.

Of course, it is not always possible to have every critical aspect of an organization's skill represented at the top. That is why it is critical to maintain faith in the fairness of the organization and a clear shared vision so that top management can get honest help from others and can trust many to act in the best interest of the company.

Maintaining and Facilitating Key Relationships. Personality differences, structural and geographical distances, and many other impediments can keep people with critical contributions to make from staying in touch. Managers must listen carefully to reports about who is getting involved in decisions and projects to make sure that the right people are involved. They must also learn to value those in their organizations who understand the know-how networks and how to use them. Recall that the top managers at Precision Instruments, discussed in Chapter Two, were apparently unaware of the tremendous value of the third founder, Harold Phelps. Not only was Phelps an excellent liaison between top management and production employees but he also encouraged appropriate problem solving between production and other parts of the organization.

At Tektronix, as I described previously, many production teams have developed critical relationships with groups both inside and outside the company. The resulting improvements in product quality, cost, and delivery time have been significant where these teams are functioning.

At Frito-Lay, some decisions about new systems must involve a broad group of people, including accounting, purchasing, sales, operations (production plants), and marketing. They have learned that the only way to avoid taking two years to work one-on-one through changes and counterchanges by representatives of each group is to have each group represented in a three- to six-day off-site meeting and hammer out the new systems' details. They meet again to approve progress at various stages. They have cut the development time for new systems in half using this process.

Thus, there are numerous formal and informal ways to encourage the right people to work together to produce the right collective skills. Perhaps the most critical aspect of getting people to cooperate is the level of trust or competition and suspicion they feel for one another. This requires that management attend to the maintenance of faith in fairness in the organization and faith in others, as discussed earlier.

Continuing to Perpetuate Skills. Skills can erode when managers cease to give attention and resources to the perpetuation of collective skills. For example, in one electronics company, managers were unable to hire new young managers for many years. Once the extended hiring freeze was over, they tried to make up for lost time. They found that, given the complex technological tasks they performed, people needed time in the organization to learn the subtasks and to gain the trust and understanding of their co-workers to comprehend and solve important problems. Even hiring older managers from other organizations who understood the technical problems could not make up entirely for lost time in the perpetuation of skills.

The most critical questions concerning skill perpetuation have to do with the hiring, training (formal and on the job), and moving of people in the organization. Managers need to pay attention to the kinds of experiences employees are having. They need to encourage the development of both interpersonal skills and critical relationships in their organizations. For example, are they willing to insist that managers in one division or department share their best people with other divisions so that people with talent develop new relationships? Certainly, short-term concerns about maintaining the quality of a particular division must be weighed against these longer-term considerations, although they must not be allowed to always take precedence. Indeed, for some time I have followed the career of one very successful manager who prides himself on how many talented people he can develop and send out to other parts of the organization. He believes that he is helping the organization as a whole but that he is also seeding the organization with people who know how to work with his group. And when these employees learn more about other parts of the organization, they will help his division relate to and serve these other divisions better.

In this chapter, we have considered very difficult executive tasks. They represent the highest form of leadership. Essentially, we have seen that those who would be leaders in developing distinctive character and competence in organizations must have integrity in helping people to understand and keep critical commitments as a group. They must also stay in touch with the beliefs and skills of the organization if they want to sustain the shared purpose and know-how. These leadership actions require significant and artful action by executives. We have seen a number of successes and failures in these tasks. This glimpse at the art of organizational leadership includes what I consider to be the most critical elements in creating a long-term distinctive character in organizations.

However, the problem is that such protection of special character and competence can lead to rigidity. How then can a firm be flexible enough to remain competitive in the face of technological and consumer changes and still maintain a distinctive character? That is the problem to which we turn in the next chapter.

8

Make the Corporate Character Adaptive: Maintaining Tension Between Tradition and Change

Not long ago, Japanese security analysts criticized the president of the largest wine company in Japan for offering a new beer product in a market that is virtually owned by three companies specializing in beer. He responded, "We have a number of wonderful young people in our company who are not learning how to learn because we already know how to make wine. I don't expect to make much, if any, money from this new beer product but it is excellent on-the-job training for our young people. I'm sure we will learn some good lessons. I'm also certain that we will be better off if we keep challenging our people to look outside the firm, explore new areas, and teach us new things."

We do not really know whether the wine company president is making a wise decision or not. He may be opening a Pandora's box of problems that the firm will not be able to cope with, and perhaps money will be wastefully diverted from maintaining and developing the integrity of the firm's character. And certainly my focus thus far has been on establishing long-term organizational commitments and preserving the integrity of those commitments.

However, the very efficiency and pride that result from the success of distinctive skills can become a rigid straitjacket that resists needed changes. Every organization, and particularly those facing competitive environments, needs to adapt. Hence, executives face the critical tension that our Japanese company president is trying to address: How can we preserve the integrity of our critical commitments and values while still adapting to the ever-changing conditions of our environment?

The role of a leader in an organization that continues to adapt and exist over time within a changing environment must be to help the organization's members consider what becomes habitual and what must be changed. Leaders in this sense will help employees see the consequences of their sometimes unconsidered choice of habits. They will help to initiate change when needed. They must not, however, overlook the importance of the organization's current commitments and skills—its character. These leaders must understand the complexity of the competence that the group has developed and must help the group learn how to learn and adapt, usually in ways that complement its competence.

Before we explore how leaders can encourage adaptation, I want to describe several ways in which the success of a distinctive organizational character can sometimes encourage resistance to long-term adaptation and effectiveness. Each of the types of organizational rigidity I will describe implies a lack of leadership. Each type of rigidity is a failure to understand and to attempt to influence what is becoming habitual. Following this discussion of organizational inflexibility, we will consider how leaders can overcome rigidity and foster a dynamic tension between the efficiency of tradition and the need for adaptation.

Types of Organizational Rigidity

Reconsider briefly the components of a distinctive organizational character as I have defined it. An organization has a character when both the ideas and the practices of its people have become ordered to some extent. That is, faith in the organization motivates people to be willing to work for the good of the organization because that seems to be in their self-interest.

Vision suggests what the good of the whole is. Faith and vision then direct the thoughts and ideas of employees in ways that motivate and coordinate their work. Organizational skills enable people to implement their ideas in distinctive and competitive ways. They develop habits and execution skills, "memories in their fingers," that make their collective efforts efficient and of consistent and high quality.

Organizations, and people, become inflexible when they lose the perspective that results from keeping practices and ideas dynamically influencing one another. For example, habits can become detached from their purpose. We engage in them unthinkingly so that we are on automatic pilot. Organizations go on automatic pilot when people assume that their past formula for success is guaranteed. Another form of automatic pilot occurs when people's thinking and ideas become locked in a static set of labels (stereotypes) that are used unconsciously. In this case, the automatic pilot is more subtle because people may appear to be acting out of their thinking. However, their reasoning and decisions are based on narrow categories and few alternatives. They do not learn things that they cannot fit into preexisting categories.

However, habits of action and of thought are only two kinds of rigidity. We have all seen, in ourselves or others, two other types that have to do with more conscious, but ideologically based, commitments. For example, we can become convinced that certain ideas or values about how to conduct business are so sacrosanct that they must never be violated. We fail to take into account the complexity and paradox of conflicting good values—like the potential conflicts among high quality, profitability, responsiveness to customers, and efficiency of operations. Or we become committed to certain practices that come to symbolize important ideas. We would never consider giving up these practices even when they become impractical. These ideological commitments can become ruts or superstitious rituals.

Although I could list an almost infinite number of organizational characteristics that constrain adaptation, I suggest that the following four are most common and critical:

1. Assuming past competence is a guaranteed formula for success (habitual action)
2. Thinking in stereotypes and labels (habitual thinking)
3. Getting into ideological ruts (ideological thinking)
4. Developing superstitious commitment to certain practices and actions (ideological action)

Habits as Guaranteed Formula. Perhaps the best example in my experience of a firm assuming that its past competence was a guaranteed formula comes from the insurance industry. Following deregulation of financial institutions, many insurance companies have discovered that they are competing with Sears and Merrill Lynch. Executives have realized that the competitive challenges they face are quite different. In this changing environment, many have seen that the previous formula for operating an insurance company has been taken for granted and assumed.

One president suggested that most people in his company seemed to feel that "God had declared there would be a profit if they just did things the way they had always done them." It was assumed that actuaries should dominate in making decisions and that the way to reach people who wanted insurance was through independent insurance agents rather than through other means of contact such as direct mail or company-employed agents. Hence, the managers in this firm tended to be passive and disoriented in the face of new challenges. They were, in the words of this company president, like the officers of a ship that had been impelled by a current who suddenly discovered that they were going the wrong way. Their surprise was doubled when they discovered that they did not understand how the ship worked. They had been giving orders and keeping busy, but they did not even know whether there was an engine or how the ship was actually steered.

The metaphor is clearly exaggerated, but the feeling that it captures is accurate. The people in this insurance company had come to assume many things about how to be successful in their industry that were now inaccurate. They had also become passive in their approach to learning new ways and implementing the old ways. They simply did what the old rules and formulas suggested. They were on automatic pilot, operating out of habit and old social conventions.

Indeed, the automatic behavior of this insurance firm seemed to result from the lack of a conscious shared vision. Most of its employees were unaware of how their efforts were related to the company's overall performance. For many years they had been without a clear idea about how their competitors and customers were changing. Their business had been successful for so long that most people failed to see a need to understand these issues. The result was a well-developed organizational skill that was disconnected from a guiding vision.

Whereas people in this insurance company had previously been unconsciously competent, the changed environment made them unconsciously incompetent. The president was trying to help them become conscious of their incompetence and then rethink their whole business so they could develop conscious competence. This is a particularly difficult problem for companies that have had prior success with a formula. The increase in pain and inefficiency when a group of people have to work through each decision and cannot take for granted previously successful ways of operating is highlighted by the efficiency of the past. We have seen this kind of pain not only in the insurance industry but also at AT&T, in airline companies, and in other financial institutions. The president of the insurance company told me that attempting such constant reevaluation was akin to rebuilding a ship while at sea in the middle of a storm.

Thinking in Stereotypes and Labels. In most organizations, groups of people who work together take on special orientations and skills. They develop a particular identity and status in the organization. While group membership can motivate people and provide the means to teach and support them, it can also lead to significant rigidity.

I have mentioned previously (in Chapter Five) a financial services firm where a group of deal makers had become the dominant group within the firm; the accountants and other staff people were seen as second-class citizens. Current environmental changes facing the firm require ideas, initiative, and leadership from people with strong financial skills, and its executives find it very difficult to change the way people in one group think about people in other groups. On the one hand, the dominant group of deal makers are not accustomed to, and do not value input from, the staff group. They have come to think of them as rule-oriented "bean counters" who are the "overhead" of their business.

On the other hand, staff group members are fond of sharing stories about million-dollar mistakes made by deal makers who neglected to consult with staff experts. However, staff members have come to think of themselves as second-class citizens who probably will not be listened to. The deal makers criticize them because they have not learned to be entrepreneurial and take risks.

Similar stereotyping can be seen in union versus management feuding within a firm wherein groups become entrenched and often misinterpret the other group's intentions and efforts. We should also recognize, however, that the stereotyping can occur with respect to the way a firm relates to its customers or its competitors. Firms that develop stereotypical and assumed categories of customers may often be surprised to learn that a competitor has found a new way to define customers. Or a firm may assume that some of its competitors are not likely to take on particular kinds of projects or develop particular products and end up being seriously surprised.

The surprise in such cases results from using labels rather than ongoing learning to come to conclusions about people, customers, or new practices. Frequently, I have observed in firms whose success has led to a "hardening of the categories" that thinking has been reduced to a dialogue of jargon. People speak in labels and are not thoughtful about the way they have gathered data and the assumptions they are making. Stereotyping often reduces faith in others and, potentially, in the organization's ability.

Using labels, rather than careful analysis, eventually reduces both the clarity of shared vision and the responsiveness of organizational skills. For example, a regional snack foods company discovered, with the help of a consultant, that it had misunderstood changes in its market for several years because it had used the same measures of number of units sold by location to determine its success. However, because it had not gathered data about competitors' prices, volume, and promotional efforts, it was in the dark. The managers discovered they had been using old analysis frameworks and data. Without enough firsthand experience, they were also unaware of subtle changes in how shelf space was being allocated. By operating on automatic pilot, they seriously limited their ability to adapt their vision and skills.

Ideological Ruts. In contrast with the habits of thought and action just discussed, some companies or groups within them have become ideological converts who would die for the cause their company represents. For people with ideological commitments, change is extremely difficult. They have committed themselves publicly and have come to identify personally with a particular way of operating. Indeed, they have made that way of operating almost a religion.

Jeff Bradley (a pseudonym) is an excellent example of this problem. Over the past six years, Bradley has created a very productive group within his organization. As a division general manager, he has been involved in almost every aspect of the design and delivery of products. He has personally sold products and has discovered a particular focus and competence for his group that had resulted in significant increases in sales every year since he became division general manager. However, the political and economic environments of the overall firm have changed. It has become obvious to many that the product Bradley has developed has a limited life cycle, and many in the firm are asking him and those in his group to invite people with different orientations into their group to produce products that differ from their previous competence.

Bradley and his colleagues have reacted with great defensiveness. They believe in their product, they "know" that it is the "right" product and that their skills are the "right" skills. They are unwilling to change. They have fought every attempt to alter their product and processes and have thus jeopardized their very existence in the organization. In addition, the time they have spent fighting the larger organization has seriously eroded their support of the product. The reputation and quality of their product have suffered significantly with commensurate decreases in sales.

In organizational character terms, Bradley's group suffers from a vision problem and has some concerns about faith. The group has lost sight of the problem of negotiating a *shared* vision and earning permission to be somewhat different. As a border guard, Bradley has sealed off his group from the rest of the organization. Although the group has continued to be responsive to environmental changes, it has not managed to convince other groups in the organization how its products continue to fit in the context of what the larger organization is trying to do. Part of the reason for the lack of willingness to renegotiate a shared vision for the division stems from a lack of faith in others and the organization by Bradley's group. It has come to see itself as unique and in some ways better than others in the company. As a result, it has been less willing to negotiate with others or to be evaluated by them. Bradley's group has ignored its dependence on the rest of the organization and has resisted requests for compromise in dealings with other groups.

Bradley, and others similar to him, have a very difficult time believing the wise counsel I once received from a manager. He suggested that it is often not as important that we do something in precisely the right way as it is that we do what we do together. As a team, we do not always need to have exactly the right play for a particular situation. However, it is critical that we are agreed on the play and that we execute it well.

In the first place, knowing what is precisely the right way to do anything in the changing and complex environment that most contemporary firms face is very difficult. Often it is more important to be united and to perform well than it is to have precisely the right product. Indeed, today's precisely right product may be tomorrow's precisely wrong product. However, when ideological commitments are made, people tend to overlook the need for tolerance and compromise; they may forget that losing today's battle may gain some progress in the overall war. Thus, motivation gained from ideological commitment is often a major impediment to change.

Superstitious Commitment to Actions. I have also seen resistance to change take the form of superstitious learning. Most of us are familiar with the rituals of some professional baseball players preparing to bat. Whether the ritual entails anointing the bat with a certain substance or a particular way of circling the on-deck box, the efficacy of those behaviors in producing better batting may be seriously doubted. Yet the batter has come to believe that such ritualistic behavior will definitely improve his chances. Some have argued that the ritual itself is not helpful in improving batting, but the confidence one has in approaching the batter's box is. In spite of their rituals, batters still fail to get a hit most of the time.

In a similar way, people in business organizations can come to develop affectations—superstitious rituals, habits, and policies. These affectations are the trappings, rather than the substance, of past successes. However, that does not mean that they are easy to eradicate. In one company, for example, it was believed that men were promoted only if they had learned that they needed to wear garters to hold their socks up.

Another example of resistant superstitions comes from a company that prided itself on being a very practical "pipe rack organization" (hanging hats on a pipe rather than buy a hat rack). It had developed a policy that it would not allow carpeting on the floors because it wanted to give the impression of a practical organization with no frills. Several managers over the years had calculated the cost of this policy and discovered that carpeting on the floors would avoid the cleaning and polishing costs for the linoleum floors and thus save the company significant amounts of money. Further, they argued, the carpets would cut down on the noise about which many of the employees complained vociferously. However, the response was a retreat to the explanation that the company had been successful because it avoided frills and that it would not add carpeting, no matter what anyone said.

These responses about the importance of garters or avoiding carpeting on the floors are a kind of means-ends inversion. That is, those sticking to their superstitious rituals identify with the means and see them as something to be maintained at all costs rather than remembering their original ends, or vision. Unfortunately, the rituals are not even critical to organizational skills required to implement a vision. When the rituals and the form become more important than the substance, rational argument and lowered performance make little difference. The problem is that people learn the wrong lessons. They learn the process, procedures, and rules and make them sacred rather than learning the principles of how the business works and developing a vision that directs efforts. The result is narrow thinking and a detachment of practices from consequences that makes the firm very resistant to change.

The theme that runs through these four kinds of organizational rigidities is that people come to assume—in a way that is either taken for granted or passionate and ideological—that their habits of thought and practice will always work. Rather than occasionally reconsidering whether habitual ways of operating have become inappropriate, people assume the validity of their traditions.

These often pathological organizational inflexibilities are largely a result of previous successes. They stem from efforts to give people a sense of meaning by appealing to a particular ideology or from the early protection of a precarious group so that its members could develop themselves and experience success. They derive from efforts to maintain stability and consistency or from a desire to give people clear symbols (like no carpets) to illustrate important ideas concretely. These are the very activities I have recommended to those seeking to establish and preserve a distinctive character.

Overcoming Organizational Rigidity

This realization—that success in establishing a distinctive character may lead to a failure to adapt—leads me to wonder whether organizational character can be established in ways that avoid these rigidities. I believe that these problems can be traced to some underlying and basic motivational problems. First, as I have stressed, people tend to resist change when they do not see that they will be fairly treated or that they can make a contribution. We have called these motivational concerns questions about faith in fairness. Clearly, some of the groups just mentioned are resisting change because they feel threatened. For example, much of the struggle between the deal makers and staff groups in the financial services company stems from concerns about loss of status for the deal makers and the lack of status of staff people. As I have argued previously, reassuring people about the importance of their role in the organization and developing faith in the organization's fairness are critical to obtaining flexible responses to needed changes.

A second motivational problem is that we find it easier to operate out of memory and habit than to consider each situation as entirely unlike previous situations. Recognizing habits and calling them into question are critical activities for managers who would avoid organizational rigidity. They should also encourage subordinates to use shared visions and broad principles rather than narrow rules to guide their organizational decisions.

Finally, many organizations punish rather than reward learning because learning often entails making mistakes. Hence, individuals are motivated to avoid mistakes and thus avoid learning. Creating an atmosphere that encourages people to make appropriate mistakes and to learn from them can curb the rigidity that results from people being ritualistic or following ruts because they do not want to risk looking bad or failing at a new approach.

The challenge for managers is to attempt to avoid rigidity by addressing these underlying motivation problems. We will consider each in turn.

Maintain Faith in Fairness. Flexibility in organizations occurs when people feel that past commitments to them and their skills will be honored or at least renegotiated equitably. I have therefore focused on how managers can honor the past and develop a shared vision. Both processes help to foster social capital that executives can call on when sacrifices are needed.

In this vein, recall the example in Chapter One of Stop and Shop, the retail firm that took time in the 1960s to train and to help people change with the times. As a result, employees changed rather quickly and, subsequently, they have had the self-fulfilling prophecy that they are able to change and adapt quickly and have felt that attempts to change will be fair to them and will give them an opportunity to change. Executive action thus has helped create a history that encourages adaptability because people are willing to make short-term sacrifices. People are willing to challenge comfortable assumptions and practices because they know they will not be embarrassed and criticized for starting the awkward process of change.

A further review of other ways to encourage faith in an organization's fairness would be redundant. Suffice it to say that the key to flexibility is that managers continually invest in maintaining the social capital of the organization by focusing on their employees' concerns of faith in fairness.

Recognize What Is Becoming Habitual. In every group of people, conclusions are made about what works and what does not, especially when the group is started or when it experiences crisis. Leaders within the group must carefully monitor these conclusions and raise for discussion those that they feel are inappropriate.

Harold Geneen, past CEO of ITT, was in many ways a very controversial executive. His driving style and acquisitions were both praised and criticized. However, his focus on looking for the "unshakable facts" clearly pushed managers to do more than superficially prepare their arguments for their proposals to him. He simply would not put up with arguments based on labels, stereotypes, or "that's the way it's done." Some may criticize what seemed to be a ruthless embarrassment of his subordinates in public when they engaged in sloppy thinking, but some observers (Pascale and Athos, 1981) make a strong case for the effectiveness of the push for "unshakable facts" in making good decisions in this setting.

I have been impressed by managers who have developed a skill in observing when others have locked themselves into narrow thinking habits. While there are many subtle ways in which a culture can create such thinking, some tell-tale signs are obvious. When thinking becomes black and white or one dimensional, for example, we have a clue that people have failed to consider several alternatives and that they are using labels rather than reasoning. For instance, when people say that something cannot be done, I have watched skillful managers curb their impulse to tear the argument apart and instead ask why it cannot be done and listen to the reasons offered. Occasionally, these reasons are the result of hearsay—conclusions drawn from stories people have heard about what has not worked and why it has not worked. Listen for such statements as, "the only way to do X is. . . ." Such statements are also likely to illustrate a "hardening of the categories." Insightful executives and managers will pay attention to such statements and the reasons behind them so they can understand what has come to be assumed.

I gave the example previously of Esso Chemicals whose executives discovered habits by asking employees in small groups throughout the company to list the rules or constraints that got in the way of implementing a new strategy they had adopted. Recall that employees listed rules and constraints in their heads that were not written down anywhere else as explicit rules for the company. They included contradictory habits and assumptions about the way the business operated. This eliciting of rules and a subsequent discussion of them led to increased willingness to explore and to experiment with alternative ways of thinking and operating that were very salutory for the firm.

Another way to monitor what is becoming habitual comes from Bonneville International, which owns a number of radio and television companies. Bonneville managers have discovered that it is very helpful to conduct entrance interviews. Human resource executives choose a sample from the new employees each year and conduct an open-ended interview with these employees after they have been with the firm for approximately six months. They ask what the employee is finding surprising, what questions the employee has about why things are done the way they are done, and how the company's practices differ from previous experiences the employee may have had.

In this way they learn a great deal from those whose experiences in the firm have been brief enough that they are still seeing with fresh eyes.

Human resource executives at Bonneville International say that they have to be careful that they do not assume that the employee understands the new culture or believe every comment. They can, however, gain insight about the aspects of the culture that are and are not being learned and particularly about the new ideas and different perspectives brought by new employees. This interview process has helped the firm step back and see itself in a new light. And it helps the company to notice what has become habitual and to consider alternatives.

Educational opportunities in many forms can be helpful potentially. However, if the only educational opportunities made available to managers and employees is technical training or training that is entirely focused on "what we want to do here," then the potential benefits for firm flexibility are lost. Although much of our training probably should be tightly focused, I do not see as many educational opportunities challenging assumptions as would seem appropriate when so many significant changes are occurring in American industry.

A number of academic researchers have developed training that focuses on encouraging "critical thinking." Such thinking clarifies and examines assumptions and explores and generates alternative thinking processes (Brookfield, 1987). Chris Argyris and Donald Schön (1978) have developed a process for teaching people to engage in "double-loop learning" through which they learn to identify, question, and change assumptions underlying work organizations and patterns of interaction.

J. C. Penney is currently negotiating a long-term (five- or six-year) relationship with two universities to provide a variety of rethinking opportunities. For example, one university will sponsor a conference every six months on specific industry topics of concern to which executives of other firms will be invited to hear stimulating vanguard thinking from industry experts. Another university will sponsor management development based on an in-depth study of the Penney culture. The express intent will be to raise for consideration many of the firm's assumptions and compare them to alternative assumptions in other companies.

Some firms have encouraged sabbaticals or leaves of absence to allow time for rethinking. IBM, in particular, sponsors executive-in-residence experiences where executives visit universities or other public institutions both to encourage liaison as well as to be stimulated by questions, alternative organizational styles, and others' expertise.

Finally, an occasional study by insiders, or with the help of outside groups, may assist management in stepping back from their daily concerns to see the firm with new eyes and to realize what has come to be habitual and assumed that might restrict the accuracy of planning, decision making, and the flexibility of the firm.

Focus on Shared Vision and Broad Principles. I have previously cited the counsel from Thomas Watson, Jr., of IBM. He suggested that those wishing to create a company that would be successful in the long run must first start with their principles or values and then seek to operationalize those values in practices that are consistent with them. Finally, they must be willing to change those practices to remain competitive while remaining consistent with their values or principles. The important point is that the principles, not the programs or procedures, are permanent. When people learn to see the constancy of principles, they become less attached to particular programs or practices.

We have already considered (in Chapter Five) the most popular story at Hewlett-Packard about how the firm avoided a massive layoff in the late 1970s. I was interested to discover that some people interpreted the story as a rule and others considered it an example of an overall concept of the business. When I collected stories at HP some five or six years after the event, everyone was able to tell me what had happened, even though many had not been in the firm at the time. However, one group concluded that the story was proof that executives had made a firm commitment that they would never engage in layoffs. These people became very cynical when in certain parts of the company, following tremendous efforts to avoid layoffs, managers nevertheless had to engage in limited layoffs.

Another group of people interpreted the story as an illustration of principles that together formed a concept of the business—a shared vision. This story illustrated to them that they had to be very careful about whom they hired and how quickly they hired people because they did not want to turn around and fire people. They wanted to develop products that would maintain a large share of their market so they could have stability for the company as a whole. They also wanted to limit their long-term debt to limit the risk of exposure to environmental and economic fluctuations. These and other practices allowed HP to take major technological risks without jeopardizing the employment of its work force. And work-force stability meant employees could feel more willing to develop long-term technological advances that otherwise might be threatening.

For these employees, the story only implied this rather complex understanding of Hewlett-Packard's vision and related principles. They believed that these several ideas could not be understood in isolation from each other. Avoiding layoffs was only possible if the research strategy, pricing, and financing principles were implemented well. The story suggested why they were interested in the whole concept. These people had a much more flexible concept of the business, an understanding that was not derived from rules or even explicit policy statements but from an underlying sense of the kind of business they were in and what it took to operate the whole business. Such broad understandings provide the kind of flexibility that cannot be obtained through emphasis on rules and procedures.

Given this distinction between principles and rules, you may find it surprising that some of the most flexible companies I have observed have some ironclad rules. I was surprised to discover that most of these rules are negative rules. That is, they are about things people must not do. However, the specific requirements of what people should do are kept at a bare minimum and are typically stated in general terms. A few clear negative rules indicate boundaries, and some general directions allow for creative applications depending on the situation.

For example, in one firm noted for its long-term flexibility, the president had said on many occasions that if anyone came to him and asked to implement a certain strategic concept that focused on market share, he would have that person fired. What he was suggesting was that his firm had a very different strategy and that anyone who was insensitive to that larger concept and asked to play a market-share game did not understand the business. Such a person had not taken time to understand what he was trying to teach.

The company also had a rule against promising a product before it had been developed. Indeed, a very well-known story in the company chronicled the experience of a former group vice president who had traveled throughout the country promising customers a particularly sophisticated new product. He generated tremendous demand for the product, only to discover that the company was unable to deliver the technology that was the key to the product's sophistication. As a result of his untimely and rash promises, this vice president was demoted and given a staff assignment with less responsibility. He served for many as an example of what could happen to people who violate this particular commandment.

However, positive rules in the culture were very general. They suggested that the company believed in developing "contributory products," products that met a need that no one else could meet (thus contributing to society). Such a product would be of the highest quality and would therefore command a very high price. The resulting large margin would "contribute" to paying back the development costs of the product within the first year. Executives taught the general idea of a contributory product by pointing to examples of contributory and noncontributory products in their history. However, the definition was broad and merely suggested a wide set of parameters within which people had great freedom to operate.

Hence, executives "put their foot down" (some call it "planting a flag") in some critical areas where they wanted to create barriers beyond which people should not go. These were the specific unacceptable behaviors of the culture. The executives also created general statements about what they were hoping to get in a positive sense, but they allowed people to operate flexibly within those broad parameters.

In the previous chapter I suggested two ideas that are consistent with this concept of providing general principles and parameters rather than specific rules. I suggested that in the day-to-day operations of the firm, managers must learn to help people "nest their vision" of the firm. When someone makes a proposal, an executive should ask, "what does this have to do with our overall purpose?" Of course, such a practice can lead to superficial rather than real understanding of the firm's overall vision. However, if engaged in carefully and sensitively, this questioning practice can help subordinates understand which initiatives fit with the firm's purpose and which do not. By requiring them in each case to think through their proposals and to try to understand the firm's external environment and keep up with changes in the firm's strategy, they come to an understanding of the business that helps them make many decisions on their own. They are also much more likely to understand the reasoning behind organizational changes.

A second idea mentioned previously is the manner in which executives deal with conflict within the firm. I suggested that conflict is most usefully resolved when managers encourage warring parties who disagree to return to shared vision and refuse to let one group win until both have understood the context and purpose of the business that relates to their difference.

By helping individuals continue to understand the overall purposes of the firm and the ways in which those purposes are changing, executives can produce much greater flexibility in the way people think and operate within the firm. However, that does not suggest that a greater understanding of the firm will help people change from one purpose to another. The focus thus far has been on encouraging thoughtfulness and on teaching principles rather than specific behaviors. But when we consider that the firm may need to make several significant changes over its history (Tushman, Newman, and Romanelli, 1986), we must consider in addition how executives and others in the firm may encourage the adoption of new competencies and new concepts of thinking about the business.

Establish the Value of Learning and Skills to Learn. Perhaps the best examples of a learning orientation are found in *In Search of Excellence,* where Thomas Peters and Robert Waterman (1982) describe a "bias to action" in several excellent companies. In these firms, the orientation was toward trying new things and making many tries rather than overplanning and spending a lot of time trying to decide what to do. Following experiment after experiment, people could see what worked and what did not work. Their many small efforts on a number of fronts provided myriad learning opportunities that help shape the direction of the company. In this same spirit is the example cited at the beginning of this chapter of a wine company president who encouraged developing a new product to require employees to learn a new business and learn how to learn.

Such an orientation to learning requires that executives in the firm be willing to have people make mistakes. I was impressed with one executive's handling of mistakes by his subordinates. He asked subordinates what information they had at the time they made a decision, and then they determined jointly whether the subordinate made an appropriate decision given the information and opportunities then available. He would often reward the manager for making a mistake and for taking the action if it seemed appropriate. If the mistake was one he disagreed with, then he would help the manager learn from the mistake and suggest how to operate differently in the future. He also was willing to tell the managers he worked with about his mistakes, suggesting that one could succeed in the company in spite of mistakes.

In another company, the top executives have a retreat each summer to which they invite two hundred people from the top echelons of the firm. Their frequent practice is to recount their biggest mistakes. Not only do they let down barriers and encourage a free discussion with their subordinates of historical difficulties and mistakes but they also encourage people to be willing to take some risk and incur the possibility of some failure. Failure is not a necessary prelude to dismissal or demotion unless one fails to learn and improve.

Lyman Porter and Karlene Roberts (1976) reviewed research showing that top managers often do not listen carefully to subordinates. Our tendency is to listen upward and talk upward. We try harder to develop a relationship with superiors than with subordinates. Paul Nystrom and William Starbuck (1984) found in their studies of responses to organizational crises that in every case some subordinates had accurately warned top management. Sometimes members of top management simply refused to pass the warnings along to colleagues. In other cases, the top group just laughed when warnings were presented to them.

But not all warnings are accurate. Which ones should managers consider seriously? Nystrom and Starbuck (1984) suggest:

1. Assume all dissenting voices have at least partial merit.
2. Evaluate the costs or benefits if the message turns out to be correct.
3. Find some evidence other than the message to evaluate its believability. (For instance, have the message bearers tried to take action in the organization that indicates they believe what they say? Are they speaking about an area of their expertise?)
4. Find ways to test in practice the warnings that might yield significant costs or benefits.

Irving Janis (1971) studied the tendency of policy-makning groups to develop "groupthink," a situation where narrow thinking and group cohesiveness lead to lack of learning and objectivity—what I have described as rigidity. He suggested that such groups (1) consider assigning the role of "critical evaluator" to each member in the group, (2) avoid stating their preference when they make policy-forming assignments to other groups in the organization, (3) routinely appoint more than one group to study the same issue, and (4) have people in policy-forming groups go back to their home group to discuss the policy group's deliberations and then report the responses back. This very deliberate procedure would be too cumbersome to use on every decision. However, requiring involvement of various points of view and insisting on rigorous challenging of assumptions and evidence are important ways to avoid hardened categories. Indeed, top management should worry if it hears no dissent. Silence often signals complacency and distorted perceptions rather than consensus (Nystrom and Starbuck, 1984).

William Ouchi (1981) suggested another practice that encourages organizational participants to learn how to learn. He observed that managers in many successful American companies were moved not only within the same function but also were given opportunities to move into several different functions or divisions within the firm. These companies tried to avoid moving people too frequently so that they had a chance to learn something in each area. But relatively frequent moves gave managers the opportunity, indeed created the necessity, to learn how to learn new ways of thinking and how to relate with others in the firm whose experience was different.

Managers who encourage learning must be willing to focus on the long term and have considerable patience in the short term. The image of pruning, introduced in Chapter Three, is apropos here. The gardener must be willing to have results that are perhaps in specific ways a little different from what was intended. The gardener encourages growth and shapes it, but does not force and precisely engineer the result. When managers work that way with people, people tend to learn self-confidence and how to learn and to create new ideas that keep the organization adaptive.

All of the preceding practices and orientations can suggest to a group within the firm that learning is valued, that mistakes can be overcome, and that it is important to learn how to learn. Indeed, employees' faith that they can contribute and that they will be given a chance to learn is a critical component of motivating faith. My additional point is that when learning becomes institutionalized, it is a part of the firm's collective competence. The firm becomes competent in adapting and learning and, hence, is better able to remain competitive and competent.

Maintain the Tension Between Convention and Change

In some ways, the foregoing discussion makes the process of developing adaptability and teaching principles (rather than rules) sound too easy. There is indeed a real tension between establishing and maintaining a clear competence and encouraging adaptation and flexibility. One executive insightfully suggested that all the current talk about creating adaptive cultures reminded him of the parable wherein an unwise and greedy man killed the goose that laid the golden egg. When executives move too far in the direction of becoming adaptive, they are likely to destroy the organization's character, a collective competence that has taken years to develop and that must be carefully maintained and protected. However, when executives move too far in the direction of protecting and defending past competence, they become prisoners of their culture.

In other words, my prescriptions can at best suggest an uneasy and complex tension that must be maintained and managed, rather than a set of rules about how a firm's business is to be conducted. No "one minute manager" prescriptions or "eight basic attributes of excellent companies" or "seven dimensions of Theory Z" will automatically or magically provide the solution for establishing a competence and maintaining flexibility over time. No "perfect" theory or concept of an organization's business can remain unchanged in the long run. In each case, broad principles and general ideas are less likely to change than are specific rules and procedures. But the leader who would establish and maintain competence over the long haul must manage this paradox and learn to tolerate the ambiguity, continually examining whether the balance between consistency with the past and charting new territory is appropriate.

I am reminded of the dichotomy William James ([1902] 1958) offered in describing different kinds of Christians. He described "once-born" Christians as those who had been born into the church and had come to take for granted their membership in that particular group. He suggested that they were often slaves of their own paradigms and rule bound and narrow in their thinking.

Others were "twice born." Such people had come to a point in their lives where they had to take apart their beliefs and assumptions and examine them critically and, having examined them, became convinced that many of their beliefs, devotions, and commitments were reasoned and were supportable.

These "twice-born" Christians were a combination of devotion and of reason and criticism. They provide a useful model for us in suggesting how people might orient themselves to the character of their organization. It is not enough to understand what has been; it is not enough to be someone who operates automatically and thus efficiently within a culture. Those who would lead the organization must not only understand and help apply the current competence but they must also understand its components and what needs to be changed and maintained. They must have a reason for their dedication to ideals of the corporate character.

In this context, I am particularly impressed with a few companies that Peters and Waterman (1982) described as excellent. The excellence movement has met with some skepticism following faddish and temporary devotion in various organizations. But the organizations I see that have taken most seriously to heart the goal of becoming and remaining excellent are companies like IBM. IBM has gone through some significant recent changes. The firm's executives have not been afraid to call people to task about forgetting basic principles. They have also been willing to rethink their character to make sure that the habits that are being formed are appropriate and to understand needed changes. This assiduous attention to adaptation and learning, as well as to understanding past competencies, is not only laudable but also very difficult to duplicate. It reflects people who are trying to do the right things rather than simply trying to maintain a posture of doing things right (Bennis and Nanus, 1985).

I see a collection of paradoxes in the leaders of such organizations. They are at once passionate and tentative. They have in mind a grand idea and link that idea to the hopes and fears of the organization's members. They are convinced that what they are doing is worthwhile and that people ought to listen and try to understand and implement what they have to say. They are also tentative and open to new ways of operating; they seek a variety of opinions; they continually try to unravel and reassemble the basic character components of their business. This odd combination of passion and humility, of belief and questioning, of a bias to action and a bias to reflection, suggests the essence of what organizational leaders must possess to sustain the character and competitiveness of their organization.

Create Corporate Character That Lasts: Honoring the Past and Changing the Future

Fortune's Walter Kiechel recently summarized the challenges executives have faced in the 1980s. "Call the Eighties the decade of restructuring: Onto the scene rode the now familiar horsemen of the corporate apocalypse—global competition, deregulation, accelerating technological change, and the threat of takeover. In response, company after company, including over half of the *Fortune* 500, restructured—shedding businesses, laying off employees, cutting costs. Indeed, one of the lessons of the new age is that such work is never over, can't be over as long as the four horsemen patrol the field" (Kiechel, 1988, p. 34). These challenges have not only created the need to change our organizations but have also threatened the character of many organizations in America.

The possibility of destroying faith in the fairness and ability of American organizations has never been as real as it is now and will continue to be in the next decade. At stake is the very soul of corporate America, as well as many public institutions that have experienced similar turmoil. My argument has been that wrenching change can destroy the character of our organizations. If we continue to ignore the commitments and skills of the past as we scramble to reach the future, then we may destroy the faith employees have in the fairness and the ability of their organizations.

To be sure, the kinds of changes we need to make require new vision and new skills. But without faith in the fairness and ability of our organizations, shared vision will vanish and corporate skills will disappear. We must involve everyone in the organization if we are to listen to enough customers, to assimilate enough of the changes in technology, and to fashion the new ideas and information into corporate skills. We are increasingly managing "knowledge workers," whether they are in manufacturing or R&D. The new competitive environments for most firms require that they continuously improve quality, shorten the cycle from design to market, and significantly improve service and responsiveness to customers. Such organizational efforts demand that employees have a clear vision of what their company should and should not do and that they be able to influence that vision over time. Without faith in the fairness and ability of their organizations to change and adapt, why should employees work on the organization's vision and internalize and influence it positively? Without such faith there can be no shared vision and thus little adaptability of the firm in the long run. Employees will be too busy protecting personal or subgroup interests to worry about the good of the enterprise.

Clearly, corporate skills also disappear with the erosion of faith in fairness and adaptability as well. In the first place, employees without faith develop self-protection skills rather than using their efforts to benefit the whole. Secondly, they fear to take the necessary appropriate risks to continuously experiment with and improve existing operations.

Hence, when faith in the fairness of the organization disappears, its future adaptability shrivels. Without faith, there is little vision and skill or willingness to create new shared vision and skills. Given the importance of maintaining or significantly improving faith in the fairness of the organization, current and recent restructurings create an enormous challenge for executives and managers. How can they make often dramatic changes while improving or maintaining faith in the organization?

I have used the notion of character and personal growth and development in this book to frame the challenges facing managers, because I think these problems require self-discipline and moral courage, the foundations of personal growth. I have recently reflected upon the parallelism between the cycles of overeating and fad dieting so prevalent in American society and the too frequent pattern in business organizations of acquisition and recent restructuring. Prior to the eighties, companies grew fat through binge acquisitions only to find that they have had to quickly divest in rather distasteful and unprofitable ways the surfeit of the past. As recent research on dieting shows, once people go off their diets they most often gain more weight than they lost (Fisher, Remington, and Parent, 1983). Part of the problem is that the body seems to recognize the binge diet as starvation. It therefore stores more of whatever is eaten as fat. Less of the food eaten is actually metabolized and used for energy—how like what happens following revolution in organizations! People recognize threat and work to protect themselves from future threat. They look busy and do work, but more of the work is self-protective. They expend much less energy to adapt and develop new skills or muscle.

In addition, a dieter usually does not develop new eating habits and self-control. When people leave diets, they return to the old habits and excesses, and the old problems return. Again the analogy is apt. Unless organizational changes develop self-control, new self-understanding, and new skills, they are doomed to cycles of continued failure.

These are the problems I have tried to address. The most critical problem facing today's managers is not how to cut costs and trim the fat. The most pressing problem if we want to significantly improve American competitiveness is how to develop and maintain employee faith in the fairness and the ability (including the "adapt-ability") of our organizations.

Clearly, we need to refocus and reenvision the mission of organizations grown too complex and too fat. Clearly, we must develop new competitive skills. But we must first honor the past if we want employees to be a part of the effort to create the future of the organization. Honoring the past includes repenting of past sins. It means renegotiating old expectations and commitments in good faith. It also means providing enough information and discussion throughout the organization so that people loyal to past traditions and relationships understand what part of the past will continue and what part must be pruned.

Some companies have found that the best way to improve or maintain faith in the organization is to avoid layoffs and work together with employees to tighten operations. IBM has made no layoffs a matter of corporate religion, and many other companies have made significant commitments to employees. Advanced Micro Devices, Bowater, Digital Equipment, Hallmark, Pacific Bell, Pacific Northwest Bell, and Worthington Industries have recently found ways to cut costs significantly without layoffs. Of course, they have had to focus on retraining and joint efforts with employees to improve efficiency (Saporito, 1987). In many cases, company experiences have been favorable, and the aftermath of renewed faith in the company has yielded significant dividends (Greenhalgh, McKersie, and Gilkey, 1986; Perry, 1986).

But honoring the past and maintaining faith in the organization do not require that there be no layoffs. Rather, they require sharing information about the real problems facing the organization, joint efforts to consider all the alternatives, and, if layoffs are necessary, efforts to help employees maintain dignity and make successful transitions (Sutton, Eisenhardt, and Tucker, 1986). Companies that ignore their past commitments, even the implied ones, to employees will lose more than employees in the layoffs and dramatic cuts in programs and costs. They may lose the very soul of their organization: employee faith in the fairness of the company.

We have considered the usually incremental and often political and experimental processes organizations have used to develop new visions. Sometimes, in the moment of clearly recognized emergency, visions announced by a few executives or managers can be galvanizing and can produce hope that leads to change. However, most often leaders of change have spent their time listening to employees, to customers, and to each other. They have tried out a variety of experimental efforts to see what works for them. They wait to announce vision when several successes and clear new opportunities make it obvious to many that the direction is real.

Hence, the development of new vision and the development of new skill go hand in hand. Corporate skills, as we saw, are most competitive and efficient when they become tacit routines executed by a large group of people. Such skills result from trial and error, from disciplined practice, and from continual nurturing. In this sense, announcing new skills makes less sense than practicing and growing them. Indeed, Marriott's CEO, J. Willard Marriott, Jr., recently commented on how difficult it is to develop and discover the real skills of a company. He said that it took the company over a decade of experimenting with a variety of business efforts to figure out that Marriott's special expertise is in running hospitality and food-service operations, building lodgings, and financially packaging the real estate involved for sale to investors. This realization meant getting out of the business of running cruise ships, travel agencies, and theme parks.

Developing corporate skill also requires maintaining faith in fairness of the firm and of others in the firm. As we have seen, corporate skills require excellent and trusting relationships between a variety of experts and others within a firm. These critical relationships disappear when employees in various subgroups of the organization protect themselves because they think they will be treated unfairly or because they do not believe that they and other employees are similarly committed to achieving the good of the company.

A Job for Border Guards

The challenge is clear. On the one hand, myriad and unforgiving economic forces are pressing for rapid change of our business and other organizations. The new management theme is to act like an "aggressive investor" inside the company, slashing costs, focusing on maximizing cash flow, and adding maximum value for shareholders (Kiechel, 1988). And the stock market seems to reward rapid layoffs and other dramatic efforts to demonstrate active concern about their investment in the company (Saporito, 1987).

On the other hand, dramatic action that does not honor the past and involve employees in joint efforts to envision a new future and develop new skills to implement that vision will ultimately create a corporate shell of little value.

Those who would lead significant change that builds corporate character must deal with these very real tensions. They must act much like the border guards I described in Chapter Six. They must live at the boundary between two (or more) groups with differing needs and orientations. They must find a way to help insiders understand outsiders' needs and interests. Change must occur quickly. They must also work with insiders to fashion a vision that reassures them about the past and focuses, inspires, and directs them in creating the future. At the same time, they must sell a vision to outsiders about what can happen and why short-term fixes will not succeed. They must nevertheless demonstrate change through movement. They must solve their own problems quickly.

At every level of the organization, we need courageous border guards who can facilitate the creation of new vision and new skills while fostering faith. They will realize that such times as these are indeed the times that can produce sterling organizational character. Individual character is formed under pressure. Every athlete knows that muscles only grow when they are challenged and required to stretch and work. Similarly, moral integrity is created and demonstrated through making and keeping commitments when it is not easy to do so. We have seen throughout this book that corporate character follows a similar pattern. What can employees put their faith in if everything is up for grabs, if nothing is sacred? What do commitments mean if they are not kept?

I believe that we stand at the crossroads in American business organizations. We must find and nurture and become border guards with moral courage to manage the real tensions we face or we will destroy the very character of our organizations.

Resources for Change:
A Guide for Assessing Corporate
Character in Organizations

When an individual undertakes to change old habits, self-insight about how the old habits work can make change much easier. Managers of a $1 billion manufacturing plant decided that their efforts to reduce costs and improve quality were leading to only small incremental changes. They began to realize that unless they made some fundamental changes they would never become competitive with their Japanese counterparts. They decided to begin a process of organizational and personal introspection to determine how the existing character of their operations contributed to their difficulties in changing and how they could best approach fundamental changes.

I was involved in the diagnosis and interpretation phases of their introspective efforts. These managers taught me how important it is to have managers involved in interviewing and interpreting interviews and observations. I have stressed the importance of this idea for some time, but this was the first group of managers with whom I have worked who took me so seriously. They teamed up with human resource professionals and outside consultants to conduct group interviews of people at all levels throughout the organization. They helped pull together observations and prioritize the areas for change. They formed task-force groups for each area and came up with opportunities for both short- and long-term changes. They also collaborated as a team on improving their own relationships and on developing an overall theme and approach for their efforts.

I could not help but contrast their insight, involvement, and commitment with that of some other groups of managers I have observed. By comparison, this group was much better equipped to lead change. In some other settings, I have felt that I was much more committed to change than were the managers in the organization.

As I suggested frequently in Chapter Two, there may be many reasons why straightforward questions about organizational character cannot or will not be answered directly and accurately. This resource is devoted to suggesting how to uncover aspects of character that are taken for granted or hidden. First, I will describe the significant challenges managers and their support staff may face in uncovering the most critical aspects of the organization. Then I will consider ways they can organize their assessment to overcome these challenges. I will conclude with suggestions about how to summarize the results of a character assessment with insights that can guide subsequent efforts to change.

Why Character Is Hard to Assess Accurately

The operating assumptions of a group of people and their normal routines and relationships with one another can be very difficult to apprehend for three reasons (Wilkins, 1983a):

1. Their normal operating habits and ways of seeing the world may be taken for granted and are therefore not something they normally discuss.
2. Even when people are aware of and able to articulate how they behave and see things, they sometimes are unwilling to admit it because they want to present the most socially desirable image of themselves.
3. Few people can talk knowledgeably about the variety of subgroups within the organization whose perspectives and habits may differ significantly.

Each of these difficulties deserves at least brief comment:

Character as Habit. Much of an organization's character becomes second nature or habitual for people who have been in the organization for some time. It is therefore difficult to assess because habitual orientations and habitual customs are not talked about (Schein, 1985). Even basic values may be taken for granted. These values are hidden in the very way we define the objects in our daily life. I have tried to help people understand this idea by asking them to define what a table is. Many start by describing something that has a flat surface and four legs. Of course, tables do not need to have four legs, or any legs at all, if they protrude from a wall, for example. After some thinking, some people will suggest that a table is what it is used for—to put things on, to study on, or to eat on. Whether or not people focus their definition of a table on the functions of a table, these functions are clearly associated in people's minds with the idea of a table. We can see that this is the case from the way people respond when I suggest functions that are not customary. For example, I suggest that a table might be used for firewood or as a weapon (for example, the legs could be used to beat people or the table could be dropped from a roof onto enemies. These increasingly ludicrous (to some) examples illustrate the point that many of us would never consider some possible uses of a table. They simply are not right to us, even though people in some cultures would think of tables as weapons or as firewood or as something to hide behind or under. This underlying sense of what is right and what is wrong, or what is appropriate and what is inappropriate, suggests orientations and values that are ingrained in the definitions we develop for the mundane aspects of our daily lives.

The character of an organization is most efficient when it is least obvious and most shared. It works to encourage and facilitate understandings between people that can go unspoken. It also helps people to solve routine problems quickly without continually having to make every assumption explicit. However, this taken-for-granted quality is also a problem when we are trying to assess the character or to fit in as a new employee.

Face Management. I observe a basic human tendency in all organizations to manage one's overt presentation of self—of one's "face"—to others (Van Maanen, 1979). For example, subordinates want to be on their best behavior when a superior approaches. We try to create a favorable impression in the minds of customers or other outsiders. Such tendencies are normal, but they make understanding real motivations and orientations more difficult. We would be surprised, for example, to hear managers admit openly that while they imply or overtly state that their concern is for employees' best interests, their real orientation is to make a profit and only be concerned about employees insofar as that concern would lead to better results. Because cultural orientations are significantly more complex than this simple statement, the statement would be, most likely, an exaggeration in any case. However, revelations of this sort are highly unusual not because they are not true but because of the desire to appear more concerned than one's deepest feelings might indicate. This natural human tendency makes it significantly more difficult to accurately describe an organization's character because we do not know how seriously to take what its members tell us about its character.

Subgroup Differences. Finally, we must take into account that every organization contains a variety of subgroups whose orientations differ from and contrast with the orientations and customs of other groups (Louis, 1983). Of course, some groups differ because they are assigned to distinct functions and provide different experiences to their members. However, I also notice in every organization a kind of natural division of labor such that a variety of people become experts in different areas. For example, some may be expert about office politics, others about relationships with particular customers, while others are expert in historical matters (they may be called "graybeards" or "old-timers," depending on the organization). Neither the content nor the groupings of experts are the same in every organization.

We also need to be aware that some employees may know relatively little about the organization's underlying character. Some lack understanding because they are new, while others have simply not attuned themselves to such matters but have focused more on technical or other more overt organizational factors.

Because of the possible variations of orientation and expertise within a company, managers may become very sensitive to one part of the organization and overlook or misunderstand other aspects or groups. The problem is that the most relevant groupings will not necessarily be the same in every organization. We must therefore be very careful to learn the relevant groupings and locate the people in each group who can help us gain accurate insight.

Thus, character is difficult to assess accurately because people typically do not know how to talk about what they take for granted, they often want us to see only socially desirable aspects, and they do not know everything about the culture and its various subcultural orientations.

Overcoming Difficulties of Assessment

How can we overcome these difficulties? Presumably, an accurate assessment will take some time and resources if managers want to capture the diversity and uncover the most important orientations and taken-for-granted habits. However, most organizations will face constraints of both time and resources. There are at least three ways to overcome the difficulties of uncovering organizational character while working within limitations of time and money:

1. Focus your assessment rather than trying to look at the total complexity.
2. Look for people and situations of contrast or crisis in the organization, which point up what is taken for granted.
3. Organize a team to conduct the study that is diverse enough to capture the diversity of the organization relatively quickly.

In Chapter Two, I suggested what I consider to be the most critical concerns to be addressed in assessing corporate character. The questions I offered may be used to help focus a character assessment on the basic components of character. Therefore, let us focus here on the second and third points in the preceding list.

Look for Contrast or Crisis. When people face contrasts or crises in their lives, they often become aware of what is taken for granted during periods of stability (Spradley, 1979). For example, some situations where we might expect contrast to bring assumptions to the surface include when people are promoted, move to another part of the company, and interact with contrasting groups or when managers or others are trying to change the behavior and attitudes of a group.

New employees and people in new settings—because of transfers or promotions—may be able to provide helpful insights about the taken-for-granted aspects of corporate character because (1) they have to learn what is taken for granted and (2) their experience in a potentially different setting gives them a clearer perspective about the setting they were in previously. People who are new to a setting often learn the "way things are done around here" by the way others respond to their mistakes. As the uninitiated bump into one after another taken-for-granted practice or belief, more acculturated employees respond by telling a story, offering advice, ridiculing, lecturing, or shunning. These responses mold the way a newcomer thinks about his or her role and about the organization. Asking newcomers about what has surprised them, or what stories, advice, or lectures they have received will indicate clues to the group's character and how it is developed and passed on to others. Of course, newcomers are not likely to have a clear sense of the meaning of everything they experience, so we must be careful to involve others in helping to interpret what newcomers unearth.

But newcomers to one setting who are old-timers from another can often be much clearer about the old setting once they leave it. Their experience in a different work environment may highlight for them much of what they previously assumed implicitly. Asking such people to contrast the old with the new and give concrete examples of the differences can help them reveal a great deal, particularly about the old setting.

Conflicts or interactions between quite different groups within a company can also highlight the orientations of the groups (Wilkins, 1983a). For example, in a computer company, I discovered that what group A said of group B most often showed me the dark side of group A's most cherished virtues and vice versa. Specifically, group A people were the technologists of the company who accused the group B management people of being rigid, only concerned with the short term, and possessed of a very superficial understanding of the company's critical technical issues. By implication, A people were celebrating their own creativity and flexibility, far-sighted attention to the long run, and deep technical insights. Conversely, B people suggest that those in group A are "fuzzy-headed, blue-sky types," while by implication they pride themselves on being hard nosed and clear minded. Hence, listening to one group describe another can lead to significant insights about the group that is talking.

Top management's behavior and employees' responses to it may also reveal aspects of the character of the organization as a whole. Top managers can potentially create crises with their demands, and their efforts to move the organization often creates contrasts with previous directions. Such managers are potentially the most visible people in the organization, and they are perceived as controlling such desired rewards as promotions, budget allocations, and work assignments. Thus, while the subgroup may have more influence on how people within the firm differ from one another, top management may have more influence on what different groups have in common.

Specifically, top managers can influence organizational character in two ways: (1) through their personal behavior and (2) through the formal systems they create. As Thomas Peters and Robert Waterman (1982) point out, if executives are consistent and persistent, they can have a significant impact on assumptions.

In terms of personal behavior, I found it interesting to

hear some of the highest-ranking executives at the computer
company just mentioned talk about their current concerns.
They frequently said that they were spending too much of their
time on short-term management details—installing and servicing
customized machines and proposing contracts, for example—
and not enough time on the "critical" long-term problems of
new product and market ideas. While many of these key managers spend approximately 50 percent of their time on concerns
related to innovation, they would prefer to spend 80 percent of
their time on new products and 20 percent on the details. The
innovative aspects of the business are the most important to
them.

In terms of systems, these executives have consciously
avoided rigid evaluation or information systems. They have, instead, encouraged a number of informal systems. For example,
the president strongly encourages division managers to hire the
ten best Ph.D.s they can get each year whether or not the company has specific jobs for them. These newcomers are then told
they have a year in which to create their own jobs. In this way,
executives communicate their high regard for innovation and
their view that bright and creative people should not be overly
constrained to fit some preexisting pattern. Instead, they should
take the initiative and create not only new technology but also
new ways of contributing to the company.

Hence, top management's personal behavior and systems
reinforce the innovative and competence-driven character of
this computer company. Furthermore, these executives' focus
is, in part, what creates the dominant subculture A and threatens subculture B.

Organize an "Inside/Outside" Team. We still need some
ways to overcome the problems of "face management" and diversity in organizations. These problems can be addressed in
part by selecting people who are known to speak their minds
and who represent various factions within the organization. Indeed, I will suggest later in this resource that in every interview
we should be asking "cultural sampling" questions. By that I
mean asking people to name those in the organization who are
experts about the issues or concerns they raise. By interviewing

"faction" representatives and "experts," we have a better opportunity to capture some of the diversity in the organization. And if these people are indeed outspoken or if the organization encourages openness, then we may also be able to address the management of face.

Another way to capture the most important diversity in the organization is to create a team of diverse insiders and some outsiders. The inside/outside team should include at least one or two key managers who will be involved significantly in guiding organizational changes. Most teams I have worked with consist of a core group of five or six people: one or two outside consultants, one or two key managers, and two or three human resource professionals. We invite other managers or subgroup representatives to meet with us as needed.

The intent is to create a group that will develop diverse and accurate insights about the culture and leave some group members inside the organization to help implement and interpret subsequent management efforts when the assessment is completed. To help surface tacit activities and reflect diversity, outsiders and insiders should play different roles. For example, outsiders are to be appropriately "dumb" and offer their observations about what surprises them and about similarities and differences with past experiences. They are also supposed to serve as "honest brokers" as the investigation proceeds. That is, they try to help insiders realize when they may have bought a party line and not considered thoughtfully what actually occurs.

Insiders are supposed to help outsiders know when they are being given a whitewash treatment of organizational concerns. They also help obtain access to various subgroups and to provide some sense as the investigation is concluding about the appropriateness of recommended solutions. Thus, an inside/outside team composed of the right people that has developed a way of working openly together can help to overcome numerous problems inherent in assessing character.

However, the team must learn to manage some potential disadvantages or problems. If the team does not include representatives of all important groups, then it should develop relationships with people within those other groups, once they are discovered, and include them as temporary team members.

A second problem an inside/outside team faces relates to its greatest strength—its diversity. That strength is also its greatest potential weakness. It may become difficult for the group to arrive at mutually acceptable recommendations. However, this problem may never present itself. The tendency in my experience is for insiders to give in and to accept whatever one or two outsiders can agree on. I have often found it necessary to teach insiders their role on several occasions and to encourage them to be thoughtful and critical and to represent their cultural point of view.

Once the team is able to elicit this type of critical review of what comes before it, however, it develops the problem of great diversity. Then the difficulty becomes working through these differences to arrive at a mutually acceptable conclusion. I have found it very useful to return to concrete data and to show how conclusions have been drawn from the data. Solutions to a team's differences often come from the observation that some people see different parts of the organization and that there should be observed differences between various groupings. The team then concludes that a small number of similar themes run through the entire organization and it becomes clearer how various groups differ from one another.

An assessment, then, starts with an understanding of the most critical components of organizational character, with ideas about looking for where the character would be most visible (for example, contrast situations), and with an inside/outside team that is organized to help capture the diversity of orientations in the organization.

Let us now consider how the role of key managers may differ from the role of inside/outside team members. I will look first at the role of managers and suggest questions they might ask. I will then discuss the contrasting role of other inside/outside team members.

The Role of Managers in Assessment

I have tried to involve managers as much as possible in the interviewing and conceptualizing aspects of an assessment even when they were not equally involved in all the efforts of the inside/outside team. The more insight managers can get into the current level of character development of the organization, the better able they will be to begin to develop it in different ways. In addition, if they hear the pain, frustration, hopes, and fears of people in their organization, then they end up being more committed to changes. The problem is to get people in the organization to open up to their managers when in many cases managers have never spent much time listening and trying to understand the character of their organization.

Managers usually cannot and often should not ask the same questions that human resource professionals or outside consultants ask. However, in almost every situation I have been in, including many where the social capital was very low, managers have been able to generate enlightening discussions just by asking a few general questions and following some simple principles about responding. Consider first the questions and then the suggestions about how to respond.

In one company, managers explained their view of the situation facing their company and the kinds of responses the firm needed to make to survive and then asked people, "What do you think will get in the way of our being able to respond to these challenges?" They asked people to be frank, sent them off in small groups to come up with responses, and then listened to the summary of group discussions.

Other helpful general questions I have seen managers use include:

1.   What do I need to know to make this organization a better place to work?
2.   If you were me [the president, the division head, a member of the operating committee], what is the first thing you would change? What would that accomplish?
3.   What are the things you would try to maintain?
4.   What is getting in the way of your doing the kind of job you would like to do?

Managers are likely to hear opinions and suggestions with which they do not agree or which even offend them. My counsel has been to avoid arguing. They need to listen to how employees see the organization. They can worry later about how to correct inaccuracies. In addition, they should also wait to compare several interviews rather than respond to one group as though it were representative in any case. Once managers understand the pattern of beliefs, they will be able to more effectively respond in ways that are not defensive and emotional. I suggest that they respond to what they hear by saying, "That's interesting," "That's helpful," "Tell me more about . . . ," or "Can you give me an example of . . . ?"

Alternatives to Interviews for Managers. Perhaps the most effective way for managers to gain insight about the character and needs of their organizations is to get out of their offices and mingle with employees. At Hewlett-Packard they call it MBWA (management by walking around). The best descriptions of this kind of management activity that I know of are in *A Passion for Excellence* by Thomas Peters and Nancy Austin (1985), particularly chapters 2 and 19. The idea is not to spy on or to try to lecture to "the troops." Rather, managers are trying to see the organization in action, understand the real needs of their people and their customers, and reinforce appropriate action in the right direction.

Let me offer several brief examples of managers who have used a form of MBWA to assess aspects of corporate character. A vice president at a major petrochemical company heard about growing product quality and delivery problems in his operation. He got up at 3:00 in the morning, donned a delivery man's uniform, and rode with several delivery trucks during the day. He got a firsthand view of the difficulties the delivery men faced and had the opportunity to listen to both customers and employees. His input, along with some other interviews and systems analysis, led to significant improvements in the quality and delivery of products. He is convinced that without his firsthand experience, the systems analysis would have led to solutions much less sensitive to the actual problems the delivery men faced.

Another manager was concerned about the quality of a huge data-processing center that was part of his operation. He realized that within eighteen months the center would be expected to handle a significantly greater load and wondered about its capacity for change and for interfacing with a more diverse clientele. He blocked out several hours a day for two weeks and found reasons to walk around the data center. He also went to the center at 2:00 A.M. on several different nights to get a feel for the operation of the graveyard shift. His rich insights about the people being hired, the structure of the organization, the physical facilities, and the processing of orders led to a complete transformation of the center and a significant improvement in the capability and morale of employees.

Other managers have used various additional means of staying in touch. John Akitt at Esso Chemicals had a monthly "lunch with John" for a somewhat randomly (and sometimes specifically) chosen group of employees or managers. One top management group conducted yearly reviews of each of twenty divisions wherein at least two or three hours were spent with a group of fifteen to twenty managers or employees answering and asking questions. In most of these examples, managers not only gained richer intuitive and concrete insights about their organizations but they also communicated a sincere concern for employees.

Interviews by the Inside/Outside Team

In contrast with managers or executives, nonmanagement members of the assessment team are usually able to ask more specific questions. However, if they only ask the questions suggested in Chapter Two, they are going to get many evaluative responses about whether or not people believe others are fair or the organization is viable. What we want to know in addition are the specifics of how evaluation occurs, what the content of the organizational competence is, and what specific beliefs people hold about the company's key competitive issues. Without a feel for such details about the content of beliefs and practices, how can managers make informed decisions about suitable business strategies and helpful ways to develop character? Certain interview skills and a particular interview process can help to uncover the specifics of organizational character. Once the specifics have been brought to the surface, the questions suggested in Chapter Two are very useful guides to analyzing the data's import.

The problem of uncovering character requires overcoming another problem that I did not describe at the beginning of this chapter. People in any organizational setting have learned that when someone unfamiliar with the culture asks them to describe what they do, the person asking does not expect a long and detailed answer and is not likely to understand the details in any case. That is, employees are aware that they know much more than they could say in a brief conversation and have learned to translate, using some general terms. For example, if I were to ask a doctor what he or she does, the answer might be "I am in obstetrics" or "I am a surgeon." That does not tell me what a surgeon does; that merely labels what the person does, and I am left to assume that my past experience regarding surgeons describes what they do.

James Spradley (1979) writes about this problem in his experience as an urban anthropologist attempting to understand the culture of tramps in a particular area of the country. Most of the sociologists who had studied these people had asked them a series of common questions. They asked them where they lived, for example. The usual response of the tramps was "We don't have a home"—by which they meant that they did not have a street address. Therefore, many articles and books written about these people called them "homeless" people. However, Spradley attempted to use anthropological methods and really understand what they meant by home. He discovered that they had a very elaborate system of finding places to sleep, of developing relationships with police, local business owners, or fellow tramps to "make a flop." Making a flop had at least 100 variations in meaning, and all of them had to do with finding a homelike situation and managing the problem of where to sleep. Most of the tramps did not feel homeless at all, but felt relatively in charge of that aspect of their lives.

Hence, as interviewers we must overcome this translation competence to get behind the labels and understand what really goes on in a person's occupation or organizational experience.

We cannot do this with any particular set of questions. Any questions we might devise would say more about our assumptions, about what is important to us, than about the point of view of another. The words we choose and the labels we use in our questions imply our own theory of organization and our own understandings.

The general strategy for interviewing, then, is not to pick a certain set of questions but to lead the interviewee into a description of his or her experience and then probe for specific examples and events and for the actual language that employees use. Unless we assiduously probe for such specifics, we will rarely discover what the world looks like from another point of view.

Following Spradley (1979), I suggest three elements in an interview that may help to achieve the goal of overcoming translation competence and arriving at more accurate and informative cultural information:

1. Establish your role as a student and the role of the interviewee as teacher.
2. Teach the interviewee how to give you specific descriptions of cultural scenes and language.
3. Get at the meaning of these events for the interviewee by asking questions that elicit contrasting meanings and ways jargon is used rather than by asking for theoretical explanations.

I will take these three elements in order and illustrate how to apply them in an interview. All three of these interview activities can be accomplished by the same process: asking the interviewee for concrete descriptions.

Establishing Appropriate Roles. Whether the interviewer is an insider or an outsider, the aim in each cultural interview is to assume that the person being interviewed is an expert in some aspect of the culture. The idea is to discover what that aspect is and then help the interviewee teach the interviewer what he or she knows. Most often, interviewees are very willing to tell us what we want to know. The problem is to teach them how to help us. I have found it useful to begin interviews with standard promises of anonymity or confidentiality of any information shared. I also describe the purpose of the particular study I am engaged in and how the data from the study will be used.

Following that, I attempt to help the interviewee understand that I am a novice and that I am very much in need of his or her expertise. I do this by expressing "cultural ignorance," usually by asking for a brief personal career history of the person being interviewed and then noting aspects of that person's experience that would be very helpful and that would make that person an expert who could help the team understand important parts of the organization. Then, as the interviewee begins to describe aspects of the organization, I can express ignorance again by saying, "That's a very interesting word that you just used. Can you give me an example of it?" Or I might ask, "Can you tell me more about that experience or event?" in probing for details, which by implication suggests that I do not know them. Taking whatever the interviewee says seriously, taking notes on what is said, and asking probing questions are all ways of expressing interest, establishing rapport, and teaching the interviewee what kinds of things are helpful to the interviewer.

Asking for Description. Asking for examples is a way of asking for description as well as ways of establishing appropriate roles. No matter what the interviewee says, we are interested not in the theories in that person's head but in a description of concrete behaviors and events of the organization and the language that is actually used. For example, if an interviewee says, "My boss is very intimidating," my typical response is to ask, "Can you give me an example of when he has been intimidating?" I have often asked people to list some words they think describe the organization, its leaders, or different competitors. When the interviewee has given me a list, I ask for concrete examples of each of these words. The more the assessment team can learn about behaviors, language, and concrete details about the organization, the closer it can get to the experiences that participants have in the organization.

Actually seeing and experiencing the daily scenes of organizational life can improve our understanding of the organizational character in operation. Interviews are a shortcut, a way to have participants summarize for us because we do not have time to personally experience every part of the organization. However, we can augment interview insights by having participants indicate what activities in their daily round might be most instructive to us. There may be typical meetings, particular production times, or particular decisions that we ought to observe in person, where possible.

Getting at Meaning. Understanding what the concrete events and details of organizational life mean to those who experience them is, in the final analysis, an act of appreciation. We try to see from another's point of view. We imagine what they feel and fear and dream about as we listen to their descriptions. Let me give an example of how descriptive questions can facilitate this appreciation.

On one occasion, when I asked for a description of behavior that would help me to understand what the interviewee meant by "intimidating," he began to describe his boss. He painted a word picture of a small, wiry man who peered through bushy eyebrows when he told his subordinate how displeased he was. The boss held a pencil and tapped it on the desk for emphasis as he spoke rapidly, criticizing the subordinate's efforts. The description was so rich that I asked the interviewee if he would show me a particular time his boss had intimidated him in that way. I asked him to play the role of the boss, and I became the subordinate. He leaned across the table and fairly shouted at me though we were within a few feet of each other. I was shocked at the language he used when he assumed the role of the boss. He swore at me, he threatened me, he questioned the legitimacy of my birth. The language he used would make a marine sergeant blush (and would certainly not be appropriate in print). I now had a completely different feeling for "intimidating" than the one I received from the word picture. When the interviewee described what he did when he left the boss's office, I understood. He told me that he went immediately to his subordinates and said that he had "just been crucified." He pleaded with them to save him from such an experience in the future by warning him about things that were going wrong in their area so that he would be prepared to answer questions.

With this description and performance, I could at least understand some of the depth of feeling the interviewee had. I also saw one perspective concerning the elements of organizational character. For example, I thought I could understand better the feelings this middle manager had about the fairness of his boss, how his boss handled mistake making (skill development), and the resulting loss of self-confidence and the increase of self-protection rather than cooperation. Of course, I could not understand the character of the organization until I included "appreciations" from other middle managers, their subordinates, and the boss.

A Suggested Process for Focusing the Assessment

Given the problems mentioned at the beginning of this resource, I have found that there is no magic number of people who must be interviewed, and I cannot specify who those people must be. There also is no precise formula for getting people to talk about character components, either because what we want to know is tacit or because people do not want to reveal some feelings. However, I have developed a general process that helps to arrive at answers to who should be talked to and what should be discussed. The process begins by assuming that we do not know for sure what the most critical groupings of employees are or what the most critical specific concerns are. (But we do know that the general concerns should relate to the components of organizational character.) What follows are the four phases an inside/outside team, in conjunction with other managers, might go through to arrive at helpful conclusions about the most critical concerns the organization faces and the best ways to begin to develop organizational character to address those concerns.

Phase One: "Lay of the Land" Interviews. The team should begin by interviewing people who are currently influencing the direction of the organization as well as people who are considered knowledgeable representatives of groups we believe to be critical in the organization. That means that we will probably interview most of the top managers and some other people at several levels of the organization. Essentially we want to learn three things from these people: (1) their view of the components of organizational character, (2) their view of the most critical opportunities and challenges of the organization, and (3) their ideas about who are the most critical factions or groups with differing viewpoints. (For the first point, refer to the questions in Chapter Two, including the change-related character questions.) Operationally, that means that managers will ask the general questions suggested previously, usually in group interviews. They also do some walking around, or MBWA. Other inside/outside team members use an interview format that includes a few open-ended questions to start (for example, "Describe the critical events in the history of this company" or "Imagine I am a new person in the company. Tell me what I need to know to fit in and do well"). The team also asks the character questions. (I often adjust them to reflect the particular situation of the organization.) As people start talking, we ask for specific descriptions.

To discover their suggestions for subject and subgroup representatives, we ask "cultural sampling" questions throughout the interview. That is, when people make an observation about the organization, we ask whether they can think of others who might have a very different view of things or who are particularly knowledgeable about key skills or key concerns they raise.

During this phase I have found some group interviews with nonmanagers to be very helpful as well. Group interviews have the advantage of encouraging multiple viewpoints and getting out more sides of issues raised than is true in individual interviews. In addition, they provide data about how people interact with one another and the actual language they use when doing so. Group interviews are particularly helpful in this early stage when the organization is large and we want to cover a broad range of groups and views before we decide how to narrow the focus for conclusions. Some members of the inside/outside team will generally check with some individuals after a group interview to get their feeling for whether the group setting inhibited or biased people's responses.

Phase Two: Initial Summary of Insights. The inside/outside team tries to summarize (1) the shared beliefs and controversies about the organization's most critical challenges and opportunities, (2) the shared beliefs and controversies about the components of character, (3) how the organization's character relates to addressing its challenges and opportunities, and (4) examples of people or groups in the organization who seem to be doing things that provide potential directions for future change.

The assessment team also focuses on determining what else it needs to understand about differences in views and values relevant to the organizational character. Which faction, topic, or skill experts do we need to see? What else do we need to know about the strategy and challenges of the organization? Armed with responses to these questions, we are ready for phase three.

Phase Three: Clarification and Probing. We return to some interviewing as determined from phase two. I have also found great insight from having members of the team tag along with people who seem to represent interesting alternatives to the way others operate. For example, in one firm we found that the productivity-through-pressure style of most of the managers was a major reason for collusion and turnover among employees. We also learned that two managers in the firm had developed very successful ways of working with employees that achieved excellent output in ways that employees appreciated; employees called it "tough love." We had members of the team follow these two managers and two more typical managers for a day each and then compared notes. What we learned was extremely useful when it came time to make recommendations. We had seen real examples that we knew could achieve necessary results in the face of actual pressures while still resolving some of the company's problems. Our recommendations were not "pie in the sky" but practical and immediately applicable.

During this phase, I have often brought groups of people together, shared the team's tentative insights, and then asked for reactions, clarifications, and suggestions.

Phase Four: Developing Action Conclusions. At this point, the team is usually ready to narrow its insights to those aspects of the current organizational character that are relevant to its business problems, challenges, and opportunities. We develop an understanding of how the current orientations and liabilities contribute to addressing or worsening the firm's problems.

We also use insights gained from asking change-relevant questions (see Chapter Two) to fashion an approach to developing the character of the organization. We review what we know about how much people share a sense of problems and solutions, the firm's experience with past changes, the most strongly shared positive values, and the company's level of social capital. In Chapter Three I offered a number of very different examples of how managers were able to begin to develop organizational character while honoring the past. Each organization is likely to develop in different ways because each starts from different situations. The problem the team faces is to develop custom-made counsel that will uniquely fit its corporation.

References

Alderfer, C., and Cooper, C. (eds.). *Advances in Experimental Social Processes.* New York: Wiley, 1978.

"AM International: When Technology Was Not Enough." *Business Week,* Jan. 25, 1982, pp. 62–68.

Argyris, C., and Schön, D. A. *Organizational Learning: A Theory of Action Perspective.* Reading, Mass.: Addison-Wesley, 1978.

Barney, J. B. "Organizational Culture: Can It Be a Source of Sustained Competitive Advantage?" *Academy of Management Review,* 1986, *11,* 651–665.

Beckhard, R., and Harris, R. *Organizational Transitions: Managing Complex Change.* Reading, Mass.: Addison-Wesley, 1987.

"Bell Battles: AT&T Marketing Men Find Their Star Fails to Ascend as Expected." *The Wall Street Journal,* Feb. 13, 1984, pp. 1, 16.

Bennis, W. G., and Nanus, B. *Leaders: Strategies for Taking Charge.* New York: Harper & Row, 1985.

Berg, D. N., and Mirvis, P. (eds.). *Failures in Organization Development and Change: Cases and Essays for Learning.* New York: Wiley, 1977.

Berlew, D. "Leadership and Organizational Excitement." In D. A. Kolb, I. M. Rubin, and J. M. McIntyre (eds.), *Organizational Psychology.* Englewood Cliffs, N.J.: Prentice-Hall, 1974.

Block, P. *The Empowered Manager: Positive Political Skills at Work.* San Francisco: Jossey-Bass, 1987.

Bolt, R. *A Man for All Seasons.* New York: Vintage Books/Random House, 1960.

Brookfield, S. D. *Developing Critical Thinkers: Challenging Adults to Explore Alternative Ways of Thinking and Acting.* San Francisco: Jossey-Bass, 1987.

Burns, J. M. *Leadership.* New York: Harper & Row, 1978.

Clark, B. *The Distinctive College: Reed, Antioch and Swarthmore.* Hawthorne, N.Y.: Aldine, 1970.

"Corporate Culture: Those Hard to Change Values That Spell Success or Failure." *Business Week,* Oct. 27, 1980, pp. 148–160.

Covey, S. R. *Seven Habits of Highly Effective People.* Provo, Utah: Steven R. Covey and Associates, 1987.

Dalton, G. W. "Influence and Organizational Change." In G. W. Dalton and P. R. Lawrence (eds.), *Organizational Change and Development in Organizations.* Georgetown, Ontario: Irwin-Dorsey, 1970.

Dalton, G. W., and Lawrence, P. *Motivation and Control in Organizations.* Georgetown, Ontario: Irwin-Dorsey, 1971.

Dalton, G. W., and Thompson, P. H. *Novations: Strategies for Career Management.* Glenview, Ill.: Scott, Foresman, 1986.

Davis, S. M. *Managing Corporate Culture.* Cambridge, Mass.: Ballinger, 1984.

Deal, T. E. "Cultural Change: Opportunity, Silent Killer, or Metamorphosis?" In R. H. Kilmann, M. J. Saxton, R. Serpa, and Associates, *Gaining Control of the Corporate Culture.* San Francisco: Jossey-Bass, 1985.

Deal, T. E., and Kennedy, A. *Corporate Cultures: The Rites and Rituals of Corporate Life.* Reading, Mass.: Addison-Wesley, 1982.

Dyer, W. G., Jr. "The Cycle of Cultural Evolution in Organizations." In R. H. Kilmann, M. J. Saxton, R. Serpa, and Associates, *Gaining Control of the Corporate Culture.* San Francisco: Jossey-Bass, 1985.

Dyer, W. G., and Dyer, G. "How Organizations Lose Their Integrity." *Exchange,* 1982, pp. 26–34.

Eldrege, N., and Gould, S. J. "Punctuated Equilibria: An Alternative to Phyletic Gradualism." In T. J. Schopf (ed.),

Models in Paleobiology. San Francisco: Freeman Cooper, 1972.

Emerson, J. "Nothing Unusual Is Happening." In J. Emerson (ed.), *Human Nature and Collective Behavior.* New Brunswick, N.J.: Transaction Books, 1970.

Fisher, G., Remington, D., and Parent, E. *How to Lower Your Fat Thermostat.* Provo, Utah: Vitality House, 1983.

Fisher, K. K. "Management Roles in the Implementation of Participative Management Systems." *Human Resource Management,* 1986, *25* (3), 459–479.

Gabarro, J. "When a New Manager Takes Charge." *Harvard Business Review,* May-June 1985, pp. 110–123.

Gardner, J. W. "The Antileadership Vaccine." Annual report of the Carnegie Foundation of New York, 1965.

"General Electric—Going with the Winners." *Forbes,* Mar. 26, 1984, pp. 97–106.

Gillan, J. *The Ways of Men.* East Norwalk, Conn.: Appleton-Century-Crofts, 1948.

Greenhalgh, L., McKersie, R. B., and Gilkey, R. W. "Rebalancing the Workforce at IBM: A Case Study of Redeployment and Revitalization." *Organizational Dynamics,* Spring 1986, *14* (4), 30–47.

Hayes, R. H. "Why Strategic Planning Goes Awry." *New York Times,* April 20, 1986.

Hayes, R. H., and Abernathy, W. J. "Managing Our Way to Economic Decline." *Harvard Business Review,* July-Aug. 1980, pp. 66–87.

Hughes, E. Z. "Angry in Retirement." In R. H. Moos (ed.), *Human Adaptation: Coping with Life Crises.* Lexington, Mass.: Heath, 1976.

James, W. *The Varieties of Religious Experience.* New York: New American Library, 1958. (Originally published 1902.)

Janis, I. "Groupthink." *Psychology Today,* Nov. 1971, pp. 43–46, 74–76.

Kanter, R. M. *Men and Women of the Corporation.* New York: Basic Books, 1977.

Kiechel, W., III. "Corporate Strategy for the 1990s." *Fortune,* Feb. 29, 1988, pp. 34–43.

Kilmann, R. H. *Beyond the Quick Fix: Managing Five Tracks to Organizational Success.* San Francisco: Jossey-Bass, 1984.

Kinston, W. "Purposes and the Translation of Values into Action." *Systems Research,* 1986, *3,* 147–160.

Kotter, J. P. *The General Managers.* New York: Free Press, 1982.

Lawler, E., and Mohrman, S. "Quality Circles: After the Honeymoon." *Organizational Dynamics,* Spring 1987, pp. 42–55.

Lawrence, P., and Lorsch, J. "Differentiation and Integration in Complex Organizations." *Administrative Science Quarterly,* 1967, *12,* 1–47.

Levine, M. "Residential Change and School Adjustment." In R. H. Moos (ed.), *Human Adaptation: Coping with Life Crises.* Lexington, Mass.: Heath, 1976.

Levinson, H., and Rosenthal, S. *CEO: Corporate Leadership in Action.* New York: Basic Books, 1984.

Lippman, S., and Rumelt, R. "Uncertain Imitability: An Analysis of Interfirm Differences in Efficiency Under Competition." *Bell Journal of Economics,* 1982, *13* (2), 418–438.

Louis, M. R. "Organizations as Culture-Bearing Milieux." In L. Pondy and others (eds.), *Organizational Symbolism.* Greenwich, Conn.: JAI Press, 1983.

McClelland, D. *Power: The Inner Experience.* New York: Irvington, 1975.

McNeil, A. *The "I" of the Hurricane: Getting Corporate Energy.* Toronto: Stoddart, 1987.

Marris, P. *Loss and Change.* Boston: Routledge & Kegan Paul, 1974.

Naisbitt, J. *Megatrends.* New York: Warner Books, 1984.

Nelson, R., and Winters, S. *An Evolutionary Theory of Economic Change.* Cambridge, Mass.: Belknap Press, 1982.

Neustadt, R. *Presidential Power.* New York: Wiley, 1980.

Nystrom, P., and Starbuck, W. "To Avoid Organizational Crises, Unlearn." *Organizational Dynamics,* Spring 1984, pp. 53–65.

Ogilvy, D. *On Advertising.* New York: Crown, 1983.

Ouchi, W. G. "Markets, Bureaucracies, and Clans." *Administrative Science Quarterly,* 1980, *25,* 129–141.

Ouchi, W. G. *Theory Z: How American Business Can Meet the Japanese Challenge.* Reading, Mass.: Addison-Wesley, 1981.

Pascale, R., and Athos, A. *The Art of Japanese Management.* New York: Simon & Schuster, 1981.

Pearce, J. A., II, and David, F. "Corporate Mission Statements: The Bottom Line." *Academy of Management Executive,* 1987, *1* (2), 109–116.

Perrow, C. "The Bureaucratic Paradox: The Efficient Organization Centralizes in Order to Decentralize." *Organizational Dynamics,* Spring 1977, pp. 3–14.

Perry, L. T. "Least-Cost Alternatives to Layoffs in Declining Industries." *Organizational Dynamics,* Spring 1986, *14* (4), 48–61.

Peters, T. J. "Symbols, Patterns, Settings: An Optimistic Case for Getting Things Done." *Organizational Dynamics,* 1978, *7* (2), 3–23.

Peters, T. J. "Management Systems: The Language of Organizational Character and Competence." *Organizational Dynamics,* Summer 1980, pp. 3–27.

Peters, T. J., and Austin, N. K. *A Passion for Excellence: The Leadership Difference.* New York: Random House, 1985.

Peters, T. J., and Waterman, R. *In Search of Excellence.* New York: Harper & Row, 1982.

Polanyi, M. *Personal Knowledge: Toward a Post-Critical Philosophy.* Chicago: University of Chicago Press, 1958.

Porter, L., and Roberts, K. "Communication in Organizations." In M. Dunnette (ed.), *Handbook of Industrial and Organizational Psychology.* Skokie, Ill.: Rand McNally, 1976.

Porter, M. "From Competitive Advantage to Corporate Strategy." *Harvard Business Review,* May-June 1987, *3*, 45–59.

Potts, M., and Behr, P. *The Leading Edge.* New York: McGraw-Hill, 1987.

Quinn, J. B. "Strategic Goals: Process and Practice." *Sloan Management Review,* Fall 1977, pp. 21–37.

Quinn, J. B. *Strategies for Change: Logical Incrementalism.* Homewood, Ill.: Irwin, 1980.

Rausch, H. R., Goodrich, W., and Campbell, J. R. "Adaptation to the First Years of Marriage." In R. H. Moos (ed.), *Human Adaptation: Coping with Life Crises.* Lexington, Mass.: Heath, 1976.

" 'RCA': Will It Ever Be a Top Performer?" *Business Week*, Apr. 2, 1984, pp. 52–56.

Rumelt, R. *Strategy, Structure, and Economic Performance.* Cambridge, Mass.: Harvard Business School of Administration, 1974.

Saporito, B. "Cutting Costs Without Cutting People." *Fortune*, May 25, 1987, pp. 26–30.

Schein, E. H. "The Role of the Founder in Creating Organizational Cultures." *Organizational Dynamics*, 1983, *12* (1), 13–28.

Schein, E. H. *Organizational Culture and Leadership: A Dynamic View.* San Francisco: Jossey-Bass, 1985.

Selznick, P. *Leadership in Administration.* New York: Harper & Row, 1957.

Signell, K. A. "Kindergarten Entry: A Preventive Approach to Community Mental Health." In R. H. Moos (ed.), *Human Adaptation: Coping with Life Crises.* Lexington, Mass.: Heath, 1976.

Simon, H. *Administrative Behavior: A Study of Decision-Making Processes in Administrative Organizations.* New York: Free Press, 1945.

Sowell, T. *A Conflict of Visions: Ideological Origins of Political Struggles.* New York: Morrow, 1987.

Spradley, J. P. *The Ethnographic Interview.* New York: Holt, Rinehart & Winston, 1979.

Sutton, R. I., Eisenhardt, K. M., and Tucker, J. V. "Managing Organizational Decline: Lessons from Atari." *Organizational Dynamics*, Spring 1986, *14* (4), 17–29.

Turner, S., and Weed, F. *Conflict in Organizations.* Englewood Cliffs, N.J.: Prentice-Hall, 1983.

Tushman, M., Newman, L., and Romanelli, E. "Convergence and Upheaval: Managing the Unsteady Pace of Organizational Evolution." *California Management Review*, 1986, *29* (1), 29–43.

Van Maanen, J. "The Fact of Fiction in Organizational Ethnography." *Administrative Science Quarterly*, 1979, *24* (4), 539–550.

Wallace, A.F.C. "Revitalization Movements." *American Anthropologist*, 1956, *58* (2).

Walton, R. E. *Managing Conflict: Interpersonal Dialogue and Third Party Roles.* Reading, Mass.: Addison-Wesley, 1987.

Watson, T., Jr. *A Business and Its Beliefs: The Ideas That Helped Build IBM.* New York: Columbia University Press, 1963.

Weisman, A. D. "Coping with Untimely Death." In R. H. Moos (ed.), *Human Adaptation: Coping with Life Crises.* Lexington, Mass.: Heath, 1976.

Wilkins, A. L. "The Culture Audit: A Tool for Understanding Organizations." *Organizational Dynamics,* Autumn 1983a, *12* (2), 24–38.

Wilkins, A. L. "Organizational Stories as Symbols That Control the Organization." In L. Pondy and others (eds.), *Organizational Symbolism.* Greenwich, Conn.: JAI Press, 1983b.

Wilkins, A. L. "The Creation of Company Cultures: The Role of Stories and Human Resource Systems." *Human Resource Management,* 1984, *23* (1), 41–60.

Wilkins, A. L., and Ouchi, W. G. "Efficient Cultures: Exploring the Relationship Between Culture and Organizational Performance." *Administrative Science Quarterly,* 1983, *28,* 468–481.

Wilner, A. R. *The Spellbinders: Charismatic Political Leadership.* New Haven, Conn.: Yale University Press, 1984.

Woodworth, W., and Meek, C. "Problems and Complexities in Implementing Participation." Paper presented at the National Conference in Employer Ownership and Participation in the Employee-Owned Firm, Greensboro, N.C., Oct. 12–14, 1984.

Wrapp, E. H. "Good Managers Don't Make Policy Decisions." *Harvard Business Review,* Sept.-Oct. 1967, pp. 91–99.

Index